HOWEVER GOD CHOOSES

He May Not Do It Your Way

Antoyne L. Green

Eleos Press

Rogersville, Alabama

First Edition

However God Chooses

Author: Antoyne L. Green
© 2012 by Eleos Press www.eleospress.com

All rights reserved.

This book or parts thereof may not be reproduced in any form, stored in a retrieval system, or transmitted in any form by any means without prior written permission of the author, except as provided by United States of America copyright law.

Cover Art: Eleos Press
Cover Design: **Create**space™ and Eleos Press
Interior Formatting: Eleos Press
www.eleospress.com
Also available in eBook form

Eleos Press publishes this volume as a document of critical, theological, historical, and/or literary significance and does not necessarily endorse or promote all the views or statements made herein, or verify the accuracy of any statements made by the Author. References to persons or incidents herein may have been changed to protect the identity of those involved.

ISBN-13: 978-0615622071

PRINTED IN THE UNITED STATES OF AMERICA

What Others Have Said

This book gives a masterful and insightful look into the life of the Old Testament personality of Naaman. Pastor Green reminds us that Naaman's experiences are common to us all and the revelation he received from God is available to us all. This is a must read for anyone facing sudden challenges, because it provides practical lessons on how to get the victory.

-Bishop Joseph W. Walker III, Senior Pastor
Mount Zion Baptist Church in Nashville, TN,
and Bishop of Pastors for the Full Gospel Baptist
Church Fellowship International

God has truly gifted Pastor Green with spiritual revelation of His word. He has given him the ability through the power of the Holy Spirit, to communicate in such a way that penetrates God's truth into the heart of the reader. Just in the very first chapter I saw myself several times. I was challenged, convicted, and encouraged by the life of Naaman. But more than that, my life was changed in a very positive way. This book is a blessing to me personally and I pray it will be to you as well.

-Sonny Schofield, Minister of Education
Lindsay Lane Baptist Church

Athens, Alabama

What Others Have Said
(Continued)

If you have struggled with your faith as most of us do, you need to read this book. Pastor Green offers great guidance and encouragement on how to effectively deal with life's unexpected "Buts." Read and be blessed.

-Pastor John. W. Jude, Senior Pastor
Pleasant Grove Church Family

In <u>However God Chooses</u>, Pastor Green wonderfully expounds that God's ways may not be our ways. However, we can truly trust His choice. I recommend this book to all that are searching for answers, as Naaman did, that cannot be solved in ordinary ways but must totally hinge on the prompting and directions of the Lord. In the midst of our "buts" and disappointments, God has a way of strategically placing the panacea to help resolve whatever our issues may be. This book is a refreshing and revealing look at how God's choices assist us in finding our deliverance and our destiny. It is, indeed, a must read.

-Overseer Daniel Richardson, Senior Pastor
Eagles Nest Ministries

What Others Have Said
(Continued)

Very simply, the most profoundly enlightening book I have ever read. I am in awe at the depth of feeling throughout this book. This work of wisdom is a course in knowing God, rather than knowing about God.

-Pastor Gary Battles
Hurricane Chapel Baptist Church

Antoyne Green has a unique style of writing. He presents the story of Naaman in a fresh way, and in a contemporary vernacular that will hold your attention. Watch out — you may find yourself in these pages!

-W. Scott Moore, B.B.A., M.Div., D. Min., author of <u>Dead Ends or Destiny: Seven Paths through the Wilderness Experiences of Life</u> (Eleos Press, 2012).

This book is dedicated to those who mean the most to me. I thank God for my parents, George and Deloris Green, and my sister, Dr. Andrea D. Willis. While I have received tremendous support over the years from so many people near and far, it all began with being reared in a Christian home where success born out of faith IN God and faithfulness TO God was the standard of living and the foundation of expectation. I'm eternally grateful for my parents and my sister.

My prayer now is to pass that same torch to my family. I'm thankful for my beautiful and loving wife, Felicia. We have three very talented and beautiful kids for whom I am so grateful-- Jasmynn, Kaleb, and Emani. These four are my life. Then, as an added blessing, I have a second set of supporting "parents." My life is enriched greatly by Reverend and Mrs. Fred Batts.

Finally, but not lastly, this book is dedicated to the greatest Church FAMILY anywhere! To each member of the New Life Church, Pastor loves you!

To everyone mentioned, I'm so glad God CHOSE to bless me by placing you all in my life.

-Antoyne L. Green
Senior Pastor, New Life Church
2314 South Hine Street
Athens, Alabama 35611

Athens, Alabama

What Others Have Said
(Continued)

If you have struggled with your faith as most of us do, you need to read this book. Pastor Green offers great guidance and encouragement on how to effectively deal with life's unexpected "Buts." Read and be blessed.

-Pastor John. W. Jude, Senior Pastor
Pleasant Grove Church Family

In <u>However God Chooses</u>, Pastor Green wonderfully expounds that God's ways may not be our ways. However, we can truly trust His choice. I recommend this book to all that are searching for answers, as Naaman did, that cannot be solved in ordinary ways but must totally hinge on the prompting and directions of the Lord. In the midst of our "buts" and disappointments, God has a way of strategically placing the panacea to help resolve whatever our issues may be. This book is a refreshing and revealing look at how God's choices assist us in finding our deliverance and our destiny. It is, indeed, a must read.

-Overseer Daniel Richardson, Senior Pastor
Eagles Nest Ministries

What Others Have Said
(Continued)

Very simply, the most profoundly enlightening book I have ever read. I am in awe at the depth of feeling throughout this book. This work of wisdom is a course in knowing God, rather than knowing about God.

-Pastor Gary Battles
Hurricane Chapel Baptist Church

Antoyne Green has a unique style of writing. He presents the story of Naaman in a fresh way, and in a contemporary vernacular that will hold your attention. Watch out — you may find yourself in these pages!

-W. Scott Moore, B.B.A., M.Div., D. Min., author of <u>Dead Ends or Destiny: Seven Paths through the Wilderness Experiences of Life</u> (Eleos Press, 2012).

This book is dedicated to those who mean the most to me. I thank God for my parents, George and Deloris Green, and my sister, Dr. Andrea D. Willis. While I have received tremendous support over the years from so many people near and far, it all began with being reared in a Christian home where success born out of faith IN God and faithfulness TO God was the standard of living and the foundation of expectation. I'm eternally grateful for my parents and my sister.

My prayer now is to pass that same torch to my family. I'm thankful for my beautiful and loving wife, Felicia. We have three very talented and beautiful kids for whom I am so grateful-- Jasmynn, Kaleb, and Emani. These four are my life. Then, as an added blessing, I have a second set of supporting "parents." My life is enriched greatly by Reverend and Mrs. Fred Batts.

Finally, but not lastly, this book is dedicated to the greatest Church FAMILY anywhere! To each member of the New Life Church, Pastor loves you!

To everyone mentioned, I'm so glad God CHOSE to bless me by placing you all in my life.

-Antoyne L. Green
Senior Pastor, New Life Church
2314 South Hine Street
Athens, Alabama 35611

CONTENTS

INTRODUCTION I

ONE: EMBRACING LIFE'S "BUTS" 1

TWO: THE MAID'S MESSAGE 9

THREE: HAS GOD SIGNED OFF ON IT? 17

FOUR: GIFTS FOR THE GIVER 25

FIVE: GET THIS! OTHERS MAY NOT GET IT! 33

SIX: STAYING OUT OF GOD'S BUSINESS 41

SEVEN: STANDING AT THE DOOR 48

EIGHT: WHEN YOUR SCRIPT DIFFERS FROM GOD'S 55

NINE: UNDERSTAND YOUR POWER SOURCE 63

TEN: CHECK YOUR COMPANY 69

ELEVEN: THEN… 77

TWELVE: PERSISTENCE DURING THE PROCESS 83

THIRTEEN: GOD WILL DO JUST WHAT HE SAYS HE'LL DO .. 91

FOURTEEN: GO BACK TO GOD 99

FIFTEEN: SO THEY WILL KNOW 105

SIXTEEN: SO YOU WILL KNOW 115

SEVENTEEN: RELEASE AFTER YOU RECEIVE 123

INTRODUCTION

Life reminds me so much of the weather—particularly in the Deep South. Take the average spring day in these parts and you're bound to see and experience the various extremes of Mother Nature in a short time period. There's sunshine at daybreak. Then it's bound to be partly cloudy and breezy by noon. Add in a steady rain early afternoon. By late afternoon or early evening, severe storms and even killer tornados can ravage the area. Doesn't this describe what we experience and how we feel some days, weeks, months, and even years? At first, everything is fine. Then out of nowhere a little trouble arises; yet we're able to overcome it. The sun and the joy that comes with it returns. Then suddenly storm clouds roll in. Winds of horror, change, disappointment, and even sorrow begin to blow fiercely causing us to feel helpless and scared. All we can do is hope, pray, and believe God for our protection, provision, and peace.

Believing in our God and what He can and will do is the fabric of our faith. It's the true litmus test of our relationship with Him because without faith it's not even possible to please God[1]. So daily, whether the sun is shining or storms are raging in our lives, we must trust God to take care of us, provide for us, and work things out for us. He's our loving Father. He can and He will make a difference in our lives. He will meet our needs. However, we must grasp this fact: our God is Sovereign. He does what He wants to do, when He wants to do it, to whom and for whom He wants to do it, and He does what He does however long He chooses. This is where our faith is challenged. Can we surrender to God when He operates differently than we ask, want, or believe He should? Like all of us at times, Naaman struggled with this. Throughout this book, if we read closely, we'll see ourselves being personified by the many shifts in Naaman's situation, attitude, thinking, actions, and ultimate deliverance. At day's end, Naaman

---

[1] Hebrews 11:6.

will teach us this one thing about being blessed: we must surrender and patiently wait for God to move as He chooses.

One: Embracing Life's "Buts"
II Kings 5:1

"Now Naaman, captain of the host of the king of Syria, was a great man with his master, and honorable, because by him the Lord had given deliverance unto Syria: he was also a mighty man in valor, but he was a leper."

Life. It can be so fulfilling and in the blink of an eye be terribly frustrating. We can be jubilant and feeling on top of the world. Then in a matter of moments we can be at the breaking point of the world seemingly being on top of us. I just saw an automobile commercial touting the most advanced braking system ever. The narrator claimed the vehicle can brake from 65 miles per hour to zero "before you know what happens." At times that is exactly what happens to us. It's also exactly what happened to a man in the Bible named Naaman. If he were here right now, he'd quickly tell us that all can be well when "before you know what happens" everything comes to a painful, stressful, and emotional halt.

A quick read of II Kings 5 and it's easy to come to the conclusion that this guy Naaman really had it going on. Life was good. Life was the proverbial bed of roses. After all, Naaman was what equates to the general, the big dog, of the Syrian army. He was well liked and respected by his superior, King Benhadad. The Lord showed Naaman and his army favor by giving them victory after victory. The text says that Naaman was honorable—that is, had clout and the respect of most people. He was a *"mighty man of valor"* meaning he was physically, mentally, and emotionally strong. Naaman was stable. He was confident and gained the confidence of those around him. Make no mistake about it. This man had everything going his way. Then a three-letter word messed everything up: B-U-T! The text spotlights and praises who Naaman was and what he was about. Then by interjecting the "but," the text aligns Naaman's life with ours as we know it.

The "but" brings to perspective the fact that no matter the progress we make in life, the productivity attached to our names, the prosperity we enjoy, or the potential we possess—no one is void of problems. The text first lauds Naaman, then lowers the boom: *"but he was a leper."*

As good as Naaman had it, he had a serious issue that he had to embrace and address. He was a leper. He had a terrible, painful skin disease. He was a social outcast. He couldn't touch people and people couldn't touch him. He was considered religiously unclean. As we'll see in a moment, Naaman didn't run, duck, and dodge. He confronted this "but" and was determined to get his life back on track.

So have you seen yourself in Naaman yet? If we're truthful, we all can relate in some way. Maybe it's not leprosy; however, each of us has been startled and stumped when "buts" arise in our lives. Some people have the big house, fancy car, the picket fence, and dream job, BUT their families are a wreck. Some people are highly respected in the community, BUT they have little respect for themselves. Some people were enjoying life to the fullest, BUT they got the traumatic diagnosis. Then there are those who had become comfortable with the peace and direction of their lives, BUT the need to care for ailing relatives arose. Still there are parents who were once proud of their children and all of their accomplishments, BUT recently the children have taken on an identity that doesn't resemble at all how they've been raised. We must beware of life's "buts."

Some things that happen to us are a direct result of bad decisions and bad judgment. The aftermath of bad or ill-advised decisions, disobedience, selfishness, and etc. are simply consequences. However, there are times when all that can go wrong will go wrong when we've done nothing wrong. Naaman was just living life while being responsible and respected when he suffered the major letdown. It's heavy upon me to tell you to stop beating yourself up about every single thing that has happened or may be happening in your life. It's not necessarily that you've made a bad decision or have been out of will of God. It could simply be that a "but" has affected your life. Every believer must realize that no amount of holiness, going to Church, tithing, prayer, reading and quoting Scriptures, drenching in oil, naming and claiming, and being Super Saint # 1 will exempt us from trouble in life. You can be an awesome prayer warrior, BUT endure extreme pressure. You can be a deacon, BUT be disappointed and discouraged. You can be the pastor, BUT be in intense physical and emotional pain. You can be the best Church member, BUT find yourself in a major mess. You get the picture. Everybody will have seasons to endure. Matthew 5:45 states, *"...for [God] maketh his sun to rise on the evil and on the good, and sendeth the rain on the just and on the unjust."* In other words, live long enough and be ready for some "buts."

So what are we to do when life shifts on us like the wind? What are we to do when we are caught blindsided by circumstances? We must embrace the "buts." In other words, we can only act as if all is well when it's not for so long. Then it's time to be real with yourself and God.

If you're hurt, you're just hurt. If you don't know what to do, you just don't know what to do. If your family doesn't feel much like one right now, it just doesn't. If your finances are in horrible shape, they just are. One can only fake it for so long. One can only lie so long. One can only act so long. We must have the attitude that says, *"It is what it is, but it's not what it's going to be!"* My son Kaleb does his homework at the kitchen table. At times he'll sit there for a long time and just stare at the paper. Finally, he'll come to me with paper in hand and say, *"Daddy, I don't get this."* Then he'll just stand there. Kaleb's simple admission to me goes deeper than five words. What Kaleb really says is, *"I can't do this on my own. I need help."* I don't know what "but" you're dealing with now. Maybe it's your spouse and kids. Maybe it's you. Maybe it's your job or sudden layoff. Maybe it is a health condition or the hard hearts of people you love. Maybe you're in an extreme season of sorrow. All you have to do is pull a Kaleb and go to YOUR Father in heaven and say, *"Daddy, I don't get this."* Then *"be still and know God is God."*

[Psalm 46:10]. God knows every pain, every situation, and every change in our lives causing us problems. He also knows just how to handle those issues. Want to know how God brings us through our "buts?" He battles "buts" with a "but." Psalm 34:19 states *"Many are the afflictions of the righteous: **BUT** [emphasis added] the Lord delivereth him out of them all."* Okay, you can praise God now! David just told us in the text that we will have troubles. However, we have a God that can and will handle ***"them all."*** Put your faith to work and speak the future over your situation right now. Your finances may be in bad shape now, BUT God will supply your needs. Your family may have forsaken you, BUT God will lift you up and Jesus will manifest Himself in your life closer than a brother ever could. Your health has taken a hit, BUT God is a healer and He will heal. Your marriage is a mess, BUT God is still working miracles. Embrace the "but" and know that God PROMISED in His Word that He'll deliver us. So when life shifts on you, stand still on the promises of God. Let me encourage you with the words of a song from

Bishop Paul S. Morton which says, *"Be blessed, my brother. Be blessed, my sister. Be blessed wherever this life leads you. Let me encourage you. Let me speak life to you. You can depend on God to see you through. And you can depend on me to pray for you! I pray for you. You pray for me — and watch God CHANGE things!"* Friend, hold on! Your change is coming!

Two: The Maid's Message
II Kings 5:2-3

"And she said unto her mistress, Would God my lord were with the prophet that is in Samaria! For he would recover him of his leprosy."[2]

God really has a sense of humor. His way of doing things often makes no logical sense to us. Maybe that's why the Word of God tells us to *"Trust in the Lord with all thine heart; and lean not unto thine own understanding. In all thy ways acknowledge him, and he shall direct thy paths."*[3] You know what this text really says? The Antoyne Green version states, *"Save yourself a bunch of headaches! Stop trusting yourself to make things happen. Trust God enough to turn everything over to Him. Then He'll turn you in the right*

---

[2] II Kings 5:3.

[3] Proverbs 3:5-6.

direction and things will turn out right." Take this text to heart because often OUR logic locks up our minds so that we're not receptive to what God is saying or doing. Sometimes the answers to our prayers and solutions to our problems are in people and places that we'd never suspect. Naaman finds this to be the case when a little slave girl—his wife's maid—has the key to Naaman's miracle!

Be mindful that God had given the Syrian army many great victories. Apparently during one of the conflicts the army *"…had brought away captive out of the land of Israel a little maid; and she waited on Naaman's wife."*[4] Please know that this is no coincidence that this young girl was captured and assigned to Naaman's wife. God orchestrated this arrangement as an answer to a problem that, at the time, Naaman didn't even have. Our God is so awesome that He works ahead of us because He already knows what lies ahead. I'm a firm believer that for those of us

---

[4] II Kings 5:2.

who trust God, some things are already worked out before we're even confronted with an issue. I believe there is a specific real estate agent with a certain property for a certain person who otherwise would not be able to purchase a home. There is a certain doctor for a certain patient with a certain disease that so far no one else has properly diagnosed and treated. There is a certain bank with a certain banker that God has on stand-by, ready to meet someone's financial needs. There is certain man or certain woman that God has been working on to make "prime spouse material" for a certain someone reading this book. The key in all of these situations (and so many others) is to be certain you have relationship with God and to be certain you trust Him in all things. Then you must listen and follow as He speaks and directs.

So God strategically plants the maid in Naaman's life. She has the answer to his leprosy. Take a look back at verse three (the text written above). The maid basically says, *"I know somebody in Samaria that can heal my master's leprosy. Gosh! I wish that he would go there!"* Who would have ever thought that a slave girl would have the answer to set such a fierce and noble warrior like Naaman free? This text speaks so much to the company that's around us. Let's look bit more closely at the little maid.

First, I love the fact that she **knew** where Naaman's cure was. She knew that God had anointed the prophet Elisha with His power to deal with this leprosy. The maid didn't "think" or "hope" Naaman would be healed if he went to Samaria. She said, *"For he **would** recover him of his leprosy."* I believe that we all need people in our lives that can do as the maid did and direct us to our help. Of course we know that our help is ultimately from God. Our help is not, never has been, and never will be in a bottle, in a syringe, in a refrigerator, in a shopping mall; in the arms and/or bed of someone God didn't place us with, or in our place depression and isolation. Our help comes from God! Therefore, we need people around us that are sympathetic enough to feel our pain, but spiritual enough to push us to God. I'll never forget when our kids were born. My wife's doctor, Dr. Hugh Bailey, calmly walked into labor and delivery. He put on his gloves, put on his "doctor's hat," and began preparing instruments on the table beside the bed. Then suddenly he began singing in such a soft, soothing tone *"There's Sweet, Sweet Spirit in this Place."* Huh? In a labor and delivery suite? Then Dr. Bailey prayed. God spoke right then! It was clear. Despite all of his medical training and expertise, the good doctor was keenly aware that he was only the attending physician. However, the Great Physician was the one who had the authority in that room. We saw that first hand after the birth of our daughter Emani in November 2007. She experienced major respiratory problems, among other issues after birth. She was in the Neonatal Intensive Care Unit for several days. If we didn't know it before, our family quickly found out that all of our help comes from God. As I said in the last chapter, it didn't matter that I was a pastor. It didn't matter that so many souls have been saved as a result of my preaching and counseling. It made no difference that my wife and I were raised in the Church by Christian parents all of our lives. It didn't matter that we tithe weekly. A "but" had broken into our lives. It was painful. It was scary. We shed tears. However, our immediate family, Church family, and friends kept pushing us to God. We prayed. I kept preaching as if everything was fine. In His set time, the Lord healed our daughter. Now she's a bright, active, and very intelligent little girl. This experience is just one of so many I could share that qualifies me to testify of the goodness, power, and love of our God. That's why I must encourage you today to trust God in all things and for all things. There is nothing so special about me or anyone else that God plays favorites. If you trust Him and give Him time, He'll provide the answer to every situation.

The maid blesses us in another way. She not only knew where Naaman's help was, she **wanted** him to be healed. It's sad, but true: there are many people who don't want to see others blessed, healed, and helped. However, this little maid not only held the key to Naaman's miracle; her heart wanted him to receive healing from the Lord. Likewise, we should surround ourselves with people who want the best for us. We should also want the very best for those around us. My heart wants you to be healed. My heart wants you to live in the joy of Jesus. My heart wants you to be saved. My heart wants you to be debt free. My heart wants you to enjoy a loving, fruitful, and rewarding relationship with that special person. My heart wants your needs to be met and your desires, according to God's will, to be given to you. That's the true creed of a Christian. We ought not to be so self-absorbed and self-centered that we don't want to see other blessed. One will never experience God's greatest blessings when jealousy, envy, and hatred brand his heart. Be happy for others as God moves in their lives. Once I was looking for a package in the mail. I couldn't wait until the mail carrier came. Finally, I saw his truck a street over from mine. It didn't matter to me that he was delivering mail to others at the time. I was excited because when I saw him at other homes it meant he was in the neighborhood. Rejoice when someone else gets the promotion. Shout when someone else's child is saved. Praise God when someone else receives the answer to their prayer. Remember, to see God moving in the lives of others indicates that He's in your neighborhood now!

Three: Has God Signed Off On It?
II Kings 5:4-5

"And the king of Syria said, 'Go to, go, and I will send a letter unto the king of Israel.'"[5]

One of the greatest pieces of weaponry in Satan's arsenal is the spirit of impulse. The enemy loves it when desperation, anger, hurt, and emotions drive us to impulsive decisions. It's during these times that we'll often take on the personality of fish and strike at the first thing that looks good, sounds good, and glitters. It's only later after we're hooked that we figure out and take to heart this simple fact: everything good is not of God! It's important that in all things—from buying an outfit to buying home to deciding to marry that special person and everything in between—that we seek the heart of God to make sure it's Him that's leading us.

---

[5] II Kings 5:5a.

This thought process is what struck me about Naaman. In the last chapter, we talked about how his wife's little maid wanted to see him healed of leprosy, so she recommended that he go to see the prophet Elisha in Samaria. Naaman gets the word that healing and help is available (verse 4). Lest I take up too much time and space, let me just reiterate to you again that there is healing, help, restoration, provision, and whatever else you need, available to you. The seasoned saints used to sing a song that said, *"All of my help comes from the Lord. All of my needs, the Lord has met and He's never failed me yet. All of my help comes from the Lord!"* Help is available to you.

In this story, after Naaman was informed that he could be healed by visiting the prophet in Samaria, the king apparently got excited. Before Naaman could say anything, King Benhadad basically said in verse five, *"What are you waiting for, Naaman? Get out of here! Go get your healing now!"* It pleased the king that his servant was soon going to be blessed. Likewise, know that it excites our King, Jesus Christ our

Lord, when we are blessed. He wants us to be blessed. He doesn't want us just to exist. He wants us to live life abundantly (John 10:10). The Lord **wants** you to be healed. He **wants** you to receive every need and many of your desires. He **wants** you to turn things around in your life so that He can receive the glory! He **wants** you to live in peace and joy. Think of this, if Christ loved you enough to die so that you might be saved, He certainly loves you enough to sustain you, take care of you, and bless you. A blessed you blesses His name. Can I guarantee the newest car? Can I guarantee a home in a gated community? Can I guarantee that tomorrow every physical ailment you have will be healed? Can I guarantee you'll find "Mr. or Mrs. Right" by this time next year? Can I guarantee a six-figure job? No. That would be very irresponsible of me to do that. However, I can guarantee that God takes care of those that are His own. Furthermore, I can guarantee that your life will be much sweeter and much more fulfilling if you completely trust God and surrender to Him.

Surrender. That's what Naaman does in regards to his king. Note in the text that the king not only told Naaman to go to Samaria to be healed, but he told Naaman that he'd write letters to the king of Israel as a sign of approval and authentication. In other words, the king "signed off" on Naaman's next move. This is precisely where, at times, we all have messed up this thing called life. We make decisions, take actions, speak, and do what **WE** think is best without our King signing off on it. That's to say that often we play God over own lives and leave God Almighty to shake his head. As you know, we live in a text messaging-crazed society now. Once I read some texts on my daughter's phone. I had no clue what they said. Each sentence was composed of abbreviated words, such as *"LOL," "LMBO," "IKR," "IDK,"* and others. I finally learned a few words so that I could text in shorthand too! The one I personally use the most is *"SMH"* which stands for *"shaking my head."* I think if God would text us, we'd see that response from Him often. I'm sure we'd get an *"SMH,"* especially when we do things on our own. Imagine it. You buy the home or car without even praying about it and end up with a high interest rate and unbearable payments. God responds, *"SMH."* You fell in lust rather than love. Now your relationship resembles a horror movie. God's response: *"SMH."* You decided to take a particular job on impulse rather than seeing what God says. Then the job closer to your home with better benefits and more money comes available. Once again, God says, *"SMH."* How many times have we gotten into trouble, found ourselves between a hard place and a rock, and ended up stressed out because we plotted our path without God's input, direction, or consent? I think you'll agree that many of our stresses, issues, and disappointments come from leaving God out of the decision-making process. The good news is that He's so merciful! Often while He shakes his head, He moves His hand and helps us in spite of us. I'm sure God hopes that we'll finally learn how to surrender ourselves, and everything concerning our lives, to Him.

Surrender. Naaman teaches us how to do it. Remember that he's the Big Cheese. He's the general of a mighty army. He's got favor with the king and the Lord. The text says he's honorable and a mighty man of valor. Still Naaman is submissive and surrenders to the king. He's a man *of* authority while being a man <u>under</u> authority. His achievements and accolades didn't erase the need for him to operate under the approval of his king. It was the king who told Naaman to go forward for his healing. We've got to learn the same lesson when it comes to our relationship with God. No matter what we achieve, how many great things are said about us, how much money we make, how many people hold us to high esteem, and how smart we think we are, we still must be submissive to the authority and to the will of God. It's simple. I want God to sign off on what I do. I want to be sure that God directs every decision. I need to know my God approves of my next action. I need to know that God is going to be with me every step of the way. That was Moses' prayer in Exodus 33:15 when he basically says, *"Lord, if you're not rolling with us [Israel] on this journey let's pump the brakes now!"* That must be our prayer. We shouldn't want to move without our Master. I should warn you that it's not an easy prayer to pray and to mean. That's because if you pray it and you mean it, and God answers it, you'll be challenged in some sensitive areas. Your desires may be denied. God's Spirit may cancel what your flesh craves. God's plan might just derail yours. In Exodus 17 Moses is looking for water for Israel to drink. In verse eight, God tells Moses to look for Him standing on the rock on Mount Horeb that would miraculously produce water. Likewise, when we really want God to sign off on our next move and lead us to our blessed place, we should ask God to allow our spiritual eyes to see Him standing on what we should be seeking. Come on, try it! Your prayer may need to be, *"Lord, lead me to the dealership that'll show me favor when buying the car, and then You 'stand' on the car that's mine."* True success is making sure that everything we do is in will of God. If that is the case, then we'll only want exactly what God has for us. We'll only seek the specific things that God intends for our lives. We need sight to look beyond the skirt and the tight abs to sense God's presence on the one we think may be that special person. We should seek God's presence and direction when choosing a college, deciding on the investment opportunity, trying to figure out wise money management, and when deciding whether or not to have the surgery. You get it. Things work out for our good when God signs off on it. This is true even if we don't understand what God's doing. We just know success follows God's signature on our lives. Why? We know because He's in control!

Four: Gifts for the Giver
II Kings 5:5b

"And he departed, and took with him ten talents of silver, and six thousand pieces of gold, and ten changes of raiment."

The other day I was working in my office at home when our two youngest children broke out into this fierce argument. From the sound of things, I knew something major was going down. Come to find out, Emani wanted some of Kaleb's chewing gum. Of course, like only a big brother would, Kaleb said "No!" I intervened and made Kaleb give his baby sister some gum. I decided this because it was the right thing to do. However, I must also admit part of it had to do with Emani having me wrapped around her finger. Anyway, I explained to Kaleb that his sister almost always gives him things when he asks. Therefore, he needed to remember that it's only proper to give back to those who give to you. Obviously, Naaman was thinking the same thing.

Naaman is now on his way to Samaria to meet up with the prophet Elisha to get healed of leprosy. However, he didn't go empty handed. The New Living Translations says that Naaman took with him about 750 pounds of silver, 150 pounds of gold, and ten sets of clothes (man, you have to feel sorry for the camels and/or people who had to carry all of this). Naaman traveled with all of this for two reasons. First, he had to cover the expense of the trip and also meet his personal needs. Then he wanted to have gifts for the man who would heal him of the leprosy. God gave me a couple of nuggets of revelation about this that will surely bless you.

First, Naaman's expectation of being healed had already created a spirit of celebration. Naaman wasn't healed yet. However, he was sure he would be healed. So he prepared to celebrate the change in his life. That's a word for you right now. The healing may not have come YET. The situation may not have changed YET. The bills may not be paid YET. Your child may not have come to his or her senses YET. You may not have been called for the interview YET. The relationship may not be upgraded from rocky status YET. The addiction may not be broken YET. Your broken heart maybe hasn't learned to love again YET. Still, by your faith, get ready to celebrate the change you've been waiting for. Naaman departed from Syria believing he would not return the same way. Today, I encourage you to believe God with all your heart that He's going to answer your prayer. Believe God that He's going to change your situation. Know in your heart that He's going to restore and revive your life. Allow your faith to lead your thinking and attitude to the point that you're ready to celebrate what God's *going to do* right now as if it is *already done!* Anyone who knows me knows that I'm a University of Alabama graduate and a loyal Crimson Tide fan. This year we won the 2011 National Championship in football (that would be the second title in three years if you count 2009…Roll Tide). My son and I were watching the title game against LSU. As soon as the game was over, Alabama players had on shirts and hats declaring the Tide as national champs. Kaleb wanted to know how they got the shirts and hats so fast. I told him that somebody believed that Alabama would win before the game even started. So they made the gear early (and yes, I know they made some LSU stuff too). In other words, they were ready to celebrate before there was reason to celebrate. That's how we must be when it comes to God. Smile. Stick that chest out. Believe the best. Speak the best. Know God has signed off of the next matter in your life. Then go ahead and make plans, by faith, to celebrate your change before it comes. You may not know how God's going to do it. You may not know when He's going to manifest Himself in your situation. However, your faith says, "GOD WILL bless me in His own time and in His own way."

It's apparent that was Naaman's thinking because he was prepared to be a blessing to the one who would bless him. He didn't only want to receive healing from the prophet Elisha. Naaman also wanted to show his gratitude to the prophet who God would use to provide the healing. We must have the same attitude. We should always look for ways to bless others, just like they look for ways to bless us. Maybe your office mate bought you lunch last week when you were strapped for cash. You didn't forget that did you? Well, think of a way that you can bless them in return. Maybe you buy him or her lunch next time. Maybe you handle a task for them when you're not busy. Maybe you buy some of their kid's Girl Scout cookies even though you've already bought 10 boxes elsewhere. Then again maybe one day you see your co-worker is down and you take a moment to pat them on the back and speak a few kind words. There are always opportunities to be a blessing to others for their kindness. However, this attitude of gratitude must also be shown to God.

As good as God has been to each of us, we cannot afford to refuse to be a blessing to Him. I know. How do you give something to our God who already owns and controls everything? Well, certainly we can't give any material thing that's going move God. However, you can bless Him with your time. Make yourself available for His work. Let me ask you something. When is the last time you visited the hospital "just because?" When is the last time you spent part of your Saturday working at the homeless mission? You can bless God by blessing others. You can also bless Him by giving Him your talents for His use. I'm blessing Him by using my gift to write in hopes of blessing others and possibly helping them move a bit closer to God. What are your gifts and talents? Use them for God's glory. Can you sing? Then do it for His glory. Can you inspire others? Do it. Can you teach and explain God's Word? Do it. Can you dance for His glory? Do it. Find a way to bless God with a talent that is uniquely yours. If nothing else, we all can bless Him and give back to Him with our praise and worship. Our praise simply says, *"Father, I remember so many of the things you've done for me and I want everybody to know it. Most of all I want to say thank you."* The mere fact that you're breathing right now, praise is in order! If you can think of just one thing God has done for you, praise is in order. Then we should also bless the Lord with our worship. Worship says, *"Father, I just love you and acknowledge you because of who you are."* Do you ever stop to celebrate God just for being God? Think of this. He's the Creator of everything and everybody. He speaks and things come into existence. He knows everything. He's everywhere at the same time. There is not one thing He can't do. He's our Healer. He's our Provider. He's our Peace. He's our everything! That's enough to simply agree with the lyrics of a popular song, *"Because of who you are I give you glory. Because of who you are I give you praise. Because of who you are I will lift my voice and say, Lord I worship you because of who you are."*

Five: Get This! Others May Not Get It!
II Kings 5:6-7

"And he brought the letter to the king of Israel, saying, Now when this letter is come unto thee, behold, I have therewith sent Naaman my servant to thee, that thou mayest recover him of his leprosy."[6]

Naaman arrives in Samaria eager to receive his healing. He meets Israel's king, gives him the letter from Syria's king, and no doubt is ready to get his deliverance party started. I'd bet never in a million years did Naaman think that Israel's king would go off the deep end after reading the letter from King Benhadad of Syria. Here's my version of King Benhadad's letter, *"Blessings King. I hear there is somebody in your area that is able to heal my main man Naaman of*

---

[6] II Kings 5:6.

leprosy. If you don't mind, please direct him to that person so he can be healed." Seems simple enough, huh? However, verse seven makes it clear that Israel's king misinterpreted the letter. Naaman is in town to get his healing. However, the one who can point him in the right direction doesn't get what's going on. Allow me once again to share the Antoyne Green translation of the king of Israel's response in verse seven. The man goes crazy and rips off his clothes. Then he begins hollering, *"Whoa! I'm not God. I don't have the power of life and death. So why is your king sending you to me to get healed of leprosy? Oh, I see what Benhadad is up to! You're his boy — his main man. When I can't heal you, he's going to attack us. This is a set up!"* Can't you just see Naaman's face? If he would have had a smart phone, you know he would've texted King Benhadad with a *"WTH!"* For those who are "textually challenged" that would mean "What the....**heck**" (smile)! Then can you hear Naaman calling Mrs. Naaman and saying, *"Baby, this guy read the letter I brought him and has lost his mind! I just need directions, but obviously he just doesn't get it!"*

Friend, you need to get something in your mind now. As you position yourself for the next matter that God wants to perform in your life, there will be those along the way that will misinterpret everything. You will face those people who will misinterpret your situation, your steps to gaining a solution to your situations, and your determination to see changes in your life. First, they'll question and form their own opinion as to how you ended up with the addiction in the first place. They'll produce their own play-by-play of how and why your marriage is on the rocks, why your children act the way they do, and why you're in financial trouble. Then as you take steps toward deliverance, the madness will continue. Some will say that you want change now only because you got exposed. Others will say that your plea for help is merely a publicity stunt to cover how pitiful they deem you to be. Still others will measure the length of your struggle and allow it to limit their belief that you really do want better for your life and to do better. However, it doesn't stop there. Some will wonder—often out loud—why you seek help and counsel from certain people, places, and things. Why did she go to that Church? Why is she going to counseling? Hmmmm, now she's holy and reading the Bible all the time. Why is he talking to *him* about his issue? Know this: your miracle is often prefaced by the misinterpreted, messiness of immature, small-minded people. It's a device of Satan to discourage you, deter you, and destroy your hope and faith that God is going to turn things around. Don't let this happen! I remember my freshman year on the basketball team at Athens High School. We had a very good team headed into what was then the Tennessee Valley Conference tournament. However, there was a team from the school formally known as Bradshaw High School. Those guys, as freshmen, were athletic freaks (and I mean that in a complimentary way). They were jumping through gym roofs, dunking as if they were in the NBA, and shooting three pointers like they were nothing. We had to play this team in the finals of the tournament. Well, we had practice the day before the game. Our

Head Coach, Randy White, called us to center court and simply said, *"Anybody who does not believe we can beat Bradshaw needs to leave the gym now! Nobody else believes you can win. That's not important. You've got to believe you'll win."* Everybody looked around. Nobody left! We knew we could win. We practiced hard. Then we went out the next day and played out of our minds. Despite nobody giving us a chance, we defied the odds and won the championship. That's what you've got to understand in life. There are some who never have and never will believe you. There are those who don't really believe *IN* you. There are those who are fair weather folks who'll bail on you when you need them most. However, DON'T LEAVE THE GYM! Stay on the floor. Work hard. Know who you are! Know whose you are! Then ask God to give you a faith that'll allow you to live and believe "out of your mind." It doesn't matter how others misinterpret or misunderstand, I believe you are miracle material. Yes, you may have to endure some folks trippin'. Just make sure YOU don't trip!

So what caused the king of Israel to get it all wrong? The Lord revealed to me that his insecurity interfered with his thinking. Naaman, the general of a successful army, was staring him in the face. Remember from earlier that the Lord had given Naaman and Syria many military victories. Also, keep in mind that Naaman was a man of high social clout. Therefore, it had to be a bit intimidating just to see Naaman and get a letter from his king. Know this: folks that have it together in God will always shake up insecure people. There are people right now that spend hours trying to figure out how you do what you do. They can't wrap their minds around how you have what you have. There are those that don't like you because you're courageous in the same situations that cause them to crumble. There are those who marvel at your strength, but in their minds they just don't get how you've survived so many things. Just know that their insecurity really has nothing to do with you. It has everything to do with the God in you. The favor, faith, and faithfulness upon your life will always irritate the fear, faithlessness, and spirit of failure upon someone else's life. So what are we to do? Do as Naaman did, and stand boldly in the authority of our King! To do so will lead to one of two things. First, it may influence and bless those around us so that they'll be eager to know our God in a very real and relevant way. If that be the case, by all means share the love of Jesus. Be practical about how you got where you are in God. Be transparent about how it hasn't been easy and how you have many, many imperfections. Certainly, be humble so you can draw them closer to our God. However, there will be those who simply will not be able to receive us and the power of God in which we walk, talk, and live. If that be the case, pray for those people. However, while staying in the mindset to **pray**, don't fall victim as **prey** to their negativity and indifference. Don't be so concerned about others "getting it" when it comes to what you're doing for God and what God's doing for you. You've just make sure you hold on to _whom_ you've got (that would be God), _what_ you've got (that would be God's promises), and what you're _going_ to get (that would be everything God has in store for you). Remember, what God has for you is just for you!

Six: Staying Out of God's Business
II Kings 5:8

"And it was so, when Elisha the man of God heard that the king of Israel had rent his clothes, that he sent to the king, saying, Wherefore hast thou rent thy clothes? Let him come now to me, and he shall know that there is a prophet in Israel."

I was flipping through the channels one day and came across the 2012 NFL Pro Bowl. This all-star game, featuring some of the National Football League's best players, was just about over. One team was preparing to kick the ball. The team's kicker put foot-to-ball and the pigskin went sailing—about five yards! It was a horrible kick. The kicker was killing himself laughing. Turns out it wasn't a kicker at all. It was Drew Brees, the superstar quarterback for the New Orleans Saints. Brees' team allowed him to attempt the kick for fun. However, one thing can't be denied. Drew Brees cannot kick! He is paid tens of millions of dollars to play quarterback. In this instance, he messed up and embarrassed himself because he took on someone else's responsibility. In our text, the King of Israel pulled a Drew Brees; except in the king's case it was no laughing matter.

In the last chapter, we saw how the king lost it when Naaman brought him a letter from Syria's king which basically asked Israel's king to show Naaman to the prophet that could heal him. The king thought it was a set up for Syria to declare war. That's why Sir Royalty got all upset, probably spouted off a few expletives, and then ripped off his clothes. The prophet Elisha heard about the king's rant and sent him a message asking why he tore off his clothes. Well, let me ask you the same question. Do you know what the underlying cause was for the king of Israel responding the way he did? It's found in six words Elisha spoke to him in the text, *"...let him come now to me."* The king was stressed and in distress because he took upon himself someone else's responsibility. Even worse, the responsibility he assigned to himself was beyond his ability! The king was right. He couldn't heal Naaman.

What have you taken upon yourself that was never meant for you to handle? What are you attempting to do that is well beyond your scope of ability? The easiest way to have a pounding headache, increasing blood pressure, ulcers, and a really nasty attitude and outlook is self-assigning stuff that you can't handle and that you're NOT SUPPOSED to handle. For some of us, it's the need to be in control of everything. For others of us, it's the zeal to serve as the "be all and end all" for everybody. Then there are those who are sincere in trying to be the best saint possible without any balance in their lives. Still there are a few folks who, whether they know it or not, give their best impersonation of God! They wanna know everything. They want a hand in everything. They try to do everything. They try to be everywhere. They do a lot often, but nothing consistently. They do several things adequately, but nothing particularly well. They get an "A" for effort and a "D" for execution and excellence. If there is one thing I've finally learned in pastoring, it's that I have to know and respect my limits and assignments. I can't appease everybody. I can't tear myself into pieces to be everywhere. There are some things I just can't do—either due to the fact that it's not my assignment or it's beyond my ability. Some problems that are presented to me aren't for me to solve. Instead, they are for me to sincerely seek God on behalf of the person presenting the issue. Think of this: your primary care physician may diagnose you with a particular ailment. Then he or she _refers_ you to a specialist. Here's the message your doctor is sending you: *"I see the problem. I care about you. That's why I'm not going to try and treat this on my own. There is someone who specializes in your situation. Go to him."* That's a message we must learn to deliver to at times. Friend, you can't solve everyone's problem. You can't change everybody's mind. You can't always make things better. You won't always have the answer. However, tune your ears to heaven's frequency and see won't God tell you the same thing that Elisha told the king, *"let him now come to me."* Please take this word to heart. I hear God saying, *"Let him now come to me with his addiction."* Maybe God's saying to you, *"Let her now come to me with her relationship problems."* God could be telling you, *"Let them now come to me with their family problems and financial issues."* You get it. Sometimes we have to love people enough to admit their issues are beyond us. We must also love ourselves enough to not allow stress and worry about others to lead us to a breaking point because of the pressure *we allow* to become a part of our lives. Learn how to recommend people to THE specialist. His name is God Almighty. The seasoned saints used to sing a song that goes, *"Have you any rivers that seem uncrossable? Have you any mountains that you can't tunnel through? God specializes in things thought impossible. And He can do what no other power can do!"* When you make this referral you'll rest better, feel better, think more clearly, and look better than ever.

Elisha spoke to the king very confidently. He said, *"Send the man to me. I'll handle his issue.*

When I do, he's going to know that there is a prophet in Israel." Was Elisha being a bit cocky? He was surely stuck on himself, right? No, not at all! I believe that Elisha was extremely confident—not so much in himself—but in the God he served who was also his source. Elisha knew that God was with him. He knew what God would do through him in order to bless Naaman. Don't ever get it twisted, my friend. It matters not how great we may think we are or how great others laud us for being. We have no ability aside from the power and provision of God. Elisha basically said, *"When the leper comes here, he'll leave knowing that God has done a great thing for him."* That's my encouragement to you. Take every single issue to God. Take the big things that keep you up at night and the little things that just nag you and make you mad straight to God. I promise you that when you turn things over to God with a heart of faith, when God gets through you will KNOW that THE God rules and reigns over all! You'll know that He specializes in turning things around. You'll know that our God has a way taking the worst situation, working it out, and leaving us to sing, *"What a Mighty God We Serve!"*

Seven: Standing at the Door
II Kings 5:9

"So Naaman came with his horses and with his chariot, and stood at the door of the house of Elisha."

I would have loved to have had a secret camera inside Naaman's chariot as he and his men made their way to Elisha's house. I can imagine that Naaman was like an excited child in the car with his parents continually asking, *"Are we there yet? Are we there yet?"* Heck, who could blame Naaman if that were the case? He was anticipating being healed. He probably couldn't wait for his skin to be baby-soft again. He was, as the kids today say, "krunk": no longer the outcast of society. Naaman probably turned up the volume on his chariot's XM Satellite radio and on came the song, *"I've got a feeling way down in my soul that everything's going to be alright!"* Anticipation should create celebration when it's God that you trust.

While certainly I used my spiritual imagination in regards to what Naaman was thinking and doing on his way to Elisha's house, I hope you got the point. When you trust God and believe in your mind, soul, and spirit that He's going to minister to you at the very point of your need, your anticipation should create a celebration within you. Faith allows us to celebrate the blessing before we see it. Faith says "thank you" before receiving anything. Faith shouts about how the situation is handled even before you see any change. Someone who has knowledge of your struggle, your pain, and your situation may inquire as to why you're jubilant in your worse times. If your faith in God is in full effect, you can honestly agree with the song mentioned above, *"I've got a feeling that everything's going to be alright."* Try it out. Think of the things you need God to do for you, in you, and through you. I assume you've prayed diligently about it. Does your heart of faith tell you that God's got your situation in control? Are you excited about what's to come? Then celebrate while you anticipate! You know, I've got a feeling that EVERYTHING in YOUR life is going to be alright!

So Naaman reaches Elisha's house, climbs out of the chariot, and stands at the front door. It's logical to assume here that since Naaman is just standing at the door, he sent one of his servants inside to announce his arrival to the prophet. Remember from the last chapter that Elisha was expecting Naaman because he told the king of Israel to *"let him come now to me."* Naaman did just that. He made his way to the prophet. Now he's standing at the door while his servant invokes the prophet's presence and the power of God working in him. It's right here that I see myself and hopefully you can see yourself as well. I can just picture myself standing on God's doorstep, hands in pocket, kind of rocking back and forth, looking around a bit—just waiting for the presence and power of my God to make the difference in my life. All the while Jesus the Christ is inside, just like Naaman's servant, talking to God the Father on my behalf. I can just hear Jesus saying something like, *"Dad, Antoyne finally made it here. He pressed his way though some very tough issues in his life. Some folks he trusted turned on him. He's had some medical issues. Then there are days, when behind a shallow smile, he's really been depressed. He needs your presence and power now."* Man, what a friend we have in Jesus! While He's not here with us physically, Jesus is in heaven now sitting on the right hand of God the Father interceding—that is, talking to God on our behalf. Friend, Jesus sees you "standing at the door." He's on the inside speaking to the Father on your behalf. Can you hear Him saying something like this? *"Dad, (your name) has finally made it here. He or she has been praying for a while. He or she is in real trouble because he or she needs help, but he or she doesn't know what to do. His or her health is not good. Friends have shown their true colors. Finances are a hot mess. It took all he or she had just to get here. Dad, he or she needs your power and presence now. He or she is here because they believe you can and will change things in his or her life."* Wonderful Jesus! We have an Advocate in Jesus Christ our Lord. We serve an awesome and all-powerful God. Therefore, all we need to do is have the determination to get to God's "door" through the study of the Scriptures, fervent prayer, our praise, and our worship. Then allow God the Son and God the Father to do the rest. Come on! Put your hands in your pocket. Smile. Rock a little bit. Look around and enjoy the beauty of God's creation. After all, you're at the door of deliverance. Things are about to change! God is able!

Eight: When Your Script Differs from God's
II Kings 5:10-12

"And Elisha sent a messenger unto him, saying, Go wash in the Jordan seven times, and thy flesh shall come again to thee, and thou shalt be clean."[7]

I'm not a fan of going to the doctor. I don't know why. Maybe it's the wait, the other sick people, the smell, the poking, the prodding, the needles, sticks down your throat, and yes, the co-pays put a very sour taste in my mouth. However, there have been times that I've felt so bad and so desperately needed relief that I forgot all of that and just went to the one I was confident could put me on the road to recovery. Of course with the visits often came numerous prescriptions, many of which never got filled. That's because I developed this attitude (I know

---

[7] II Kings 5:10.

you've never done this) that all the prescriptions weren't necessary and that I could develop my own treatment regimen that would certainly bring about a healing soon—and for less money! In the end, there have been times my symptoms got worse, I ached longer, got more frustrated, and I ended up back in the doctor's office again. That's because I did my thing because his plan of treatment didn't match mine. His way was different from mine. Never mind I was the one who went to him. That signaled I supposedly trusted my doctor. Never mind that he's the one who had the expertise. Most of us have problems with others and even with God when our script for things concerning our lives doesn't gel with theirs. I hear Naaman shouting *"Amen!"*

Naaman had been waiting at the door for the prophet Elisha to come out and heal him of leprosy. After all, everybody said he could and would. The prophet even sent word to the king of Israel to send Naaman to him. So, in Naaman's mind, deliverance is just an open door away. Well, the door does open. However, it's not Elisha. It's his servant with some unusual instructions. Again, the Antoyne Green version reads this way, *"Umm, Elisha told me to tell you to run down to the Jordan River. When you get there, baptize yourself seven times. When you get finished, your skin will be smooth and silky. Thanks for coming. Hit me up on Twitter to let me know you're straight!"* Can you just imagine Naaman's mouth dropping and his eyes as huge as silver dollars? This certainly was not Naaman's picture of how this healing and deliverance were going to take place. It takes Naaman back. It makes him mad. In fact, he's furious. In verses 11 and 12 he basically says, *"My God! I came all this way to see this man. The least he could've done is to come outside, stand beside me, pray to the Lord, and wave his hands over the place. Then I'd be healed. Instead, this man didn't even come outside. He sent his servant to tell me to go wash in Jordan River. If I **had** to go to a river, surely he could've sent me to the clean and fresh waters of Damascus. Those rivers are far better than all the rivers in Israel. Heck! Forget it! I'm out of here!"* Bottom line, Naaman throws a tantrum because things didn't go as *HE* had planned. His script for the healing didn't match Elisha's and, ultimately, God's script.

Now, before we throw Naaman under the bus, all of us have had times when God's process has thrown us for a loop. Sometimes we inadvertently treat God as a parent would treat a child. We want Him to do what we want, how we want, and when we want. We forget that He's OUR Creator and Master and not the other way around. Therefore, God has the sovereign prerogative to do what He wants and how he wants. He owes us no explanation. While He's gracious to answer so many of our prayers, He's not required to conform to us and our plans for one minute. The Bible is clear that God's thoughts are not our thoughts and His ways are not our ways. [8] Therefore, when our plans, agendas, and scripts for our lives clash with God's, somebody has got to be submissive. Somebody has to deny himself. Somebody must relinquish control to the other. That somebody is me. That somebody is you.

---

[8] Isaiah 55:8-9.

Consider the fact that Naaman traveled all the way to Samaria to be healed. He had just gotten the prescription for the healing. However, he was just like me after the leaving the doctor's office. Naaman had his own treatment plan. One would think that after enduring the physical, emotional, and mental pain associated with leprosy that Naaman would have just delighted in the words, *"and thou shalt be clean."* What Naaman came for was about to happen—IF he could only deny himself and continue to trust God even when the Lord's plan doesn't make sense to him. Friend, long nights will get longer and stresses will get far more intense than necessary the more you refute God's plan. You wanted the house. However, God arranged for you to get the apartment first. You wanted to be married by now. However, God hasn't sent the right person yet. That means the more you try to make a relationship be the big love affair, the end result remains the same—it fizzles. You wanted out of your relationship. However, God has told you to hang in there because He's turning things around. You wanted to take more money in job offer # 1. However, God directed you to take less money and accept job offer # 2. You want a miraculous healing. Yet God's plan is for you to take medicines, endure intense rehab, and gain your healing day-by-day. You're ready for a fresh start NOW. Still God says He's not through with you in your current place. You want to "will" yourself into feeling better and instantly thinking differently. Yet God wants to walk you through a slow process of recovery. All of us endure periods in which God's choice is not ours and God's agenda is far from ours. This is where walking by faith and not by sight comes in.[9] This is where believing that God really is working things together for our good comes in.[10] Most of all, this is where obedience to God's direction comes in.

Chances are fairly good that you own and use a GPS system when driving. These things are

---

[9] II Corinthians 5:7.

[10] Romans 8:28.

so cool because street-by-street and turn-by-turn they have a unique way of directing us to the right place. They know exactly where we are. They know the speed we're traveling. When we miss a turn, they know how to recalculate our routes so we can keep going. GPS systems are so unique because basically there's a satellite in the sky that's tracking our every move. Likewise, we have a loving God stationed high above us that's tracking our every move. Like the GPS, God wants to direct our lives turn-by-turn. You're still here and I'm still here because God has recalculated our routes so many times when we've gone astray, made mistakes, and followed our own plan. Furthermore, God knows exactly where we are in our lives at all times. Therefore, it makes sense to trust Him even when His directions don't make sense to us. I trust my GPS so much that I turn in strange places, I change lanes when I'm told, and I slow down when I hear it say, *"caution."* Now, I trust a computer and a satellite, both of which are made and programmed by men to lead me all the time. That being the case, it just makes sense to me that I'd trust the God who sits higher than every satellite and is the maker of the men who made the satellite. We don't have to *underline*understand*underline* God. However, in our minds, hearts, and spirits we must be submissive to the point that we're always comfortable *underline*underneath*underline* His Holy shadow.

Nine: Understand Your Power Source
II Kings 5:10

So I was excited to finish Chapter Eight of this book and was ready to move to the next part of Naaman's story when the Lord pumped the brakes on my writing. I was talking to a friend when the Lord spoke clearly, *"Son, you haven't finished dealing with verse 10 yet."* I was like, *"Okay, what did I miss?"* The Lord redacted, *"You've got to lead them to understanding their power source."* So, here it goes. Friend, everything you need for your deliverance is really within in you now. That was the case with Naaman. However, either he didn't know it or he ignored it. Let me explain.

Fact: Naaman went to Samaria so Elisha could heal him of leprosy. Fact: The prophet Elisha was certainly a man of God who was full of faith and power. Fact: Naaman obviously had faith in Elisha and the power within in him to deal with the leprosy. That's why he went to him. Fact: Naaman got upset when Elisha didn't come outside to see him and sent him what had to seem like absurd directions to go wash in the Jordan River. Okay, I hear you, *"I know this. Now tell me what I don't know."* Fact: Nothing in Elisha himself would make the healing take place. Fact: Nothing in the Jordan River or the Abana and Pharpar Rivers that Naaman preferred to go to (if he just had to) had healing properties. **Fact: whether or not Naaman would be healed was totally contingent upon what was — or wasn't — inside of him.** Let's try it this way. I was working on a science project with our son Kaleb. It was a project that produces chemical reactions from simple, household projects. The gist of the project was easy. Put baking soda in a cup. Then put liquid soap in the same cup. Follow that with the juice of a lemon. Then stir. Suddenly, bubbles start flowing out of the cup. The alkaline base provided by the baking soda reacts with the citric acid from the lemon. When stirred the result is carbon dioxide gas which creates the bubbles from the soap. All of this happened from simple ingredients coming together in one place. What would have happened if faith, humility, and obedience had mixed in Naaman's heart? Joy, even though he didn't understand his instructions, would have bubbled over inside of Naaman. Then he would've gone to the Jordan, dipped, and gotten delivered. Likewise, what happens if faith, humility, and obedience are combined in our hearts and are stirred by the Holy Spirit? Then joy, peace, expectation, and praise will bubble out uncontrollably until our deliverance, healing, provision, and etc. come forth.

Please get this! Our faith, humility, and obedience form the plug that connects us to God's presence, power, and provision. Help is available. Healing is available. Deliverance is available. Restoration is available. Provision for all of our needs is available. The key is plugging into God. I want you to try something. Take your vacuum cleaner and set it beside a wall outlet plug. Now turn it on and vacuum the floor. What? It won't run? Well, call the utilities company to fix the plug. What? There's nothing wrong with the plug because the lamp is plugged in and its light is on? Oh, I get it. You didn't plug the vacuum into the socket; therefore, you didn't use the power that's available to you. You've got it now! Could it be that you didn't do well on the job interview because you spoke without plugging into God? Could it be that you got a bad deal because you negotiated out of desperation rather than plugging into God? Could it be that healing is available, but you're still hurting because you've yet to plug into God? Could it be that you're about to lose your mind on stuff that really doesn't matter because you're sitting there, powerless? Could it be that what you've prayed so hard for has yielded nothing because your prayer was without power and you're living each day without power? That's to say that your faith, humility, and spirit of obedience haven't had a Holy Ghost reaction yet. Ask God to stir up what's within you so you plug into the power. Then you can walk, talk, and live in the power of our Almighty God.

Your power source is not resting in other people. Your power source is not resting in things, places, and possessions. Your power source is God all by Himself. That's why we must plug into Him. Then when we do, He'll empower us and enlighten us in regards to the next matter in our lives. Few of us call our local utilities company and ask for intricate details on how the power is manufactured, where it comes from, and etc. We just plug into the socket and enjoy the power. We must see God the same way. Don't be so concerned about how God does things. Just plug into Him and enjoy the light, warmth, and other blessings of being so close to Him.

Ten: Check Your Company
II Kings 5:13

"And his servants came near, and spake unto him, and said, My father, if the prophet had bid thee do some great thing, wouldest thou not have done it? How much rather then, when he saith to thee, Wash, and be clean?"

I have always loved big machines. As a kid, I would sit for hours at my grandparents' house and watch as farmers and their big tractors worked the surrounding land. Even now, I'm enthralled by huge tractors, trucks, buses, and etc. I know it sounds silly. However, there's nothing wrong with allowing the kid on the inside of us to smile and have a few "wow" moments on occasion. One thing I actually get a kick out of watching these days is the garbage truck. Yes, the darn garbage truck! It's amazing how God inspires men to invent some amazing stuff. Now the garbage itself does nothing for me! However, watching the truck drive up to the curb, swing out this big mechanical arm, pick up my heavy can, dump all my garbage, and then set the can back down is intriguing to me. So much so that, a couple of summers ago, I was outside working in the yard when the garbage truck came. This time, two men jumped off the back of the truck and manually dumped my can. The same thing happened the next week. The new truck came and I was kind of bummed out about it. I murmured out loud, *"Ah man, they've gotten rid of my truck."* My daughter Jasmynn replied, *"What's the difference as long as the garbage is picked up?"* She had a point! The important thing is that the garbage was no longer at my house. It really didn't matter how the men took it; as long as they did! Sometimes in life, we develop within our minds this long, intricate, detailed, and ceremonial way that God should handle things. Then we get bent out of shape when God chooses to do things another way. It's at those times that we must really refocus and grasp what's most important: the _manifestation_ of the blessing and NOT necessarily the _method_ God chooses to bestow the blessings. It's a lesson we must learn. It's a lesson apparently Naaman needed to learn.

Naaman had just thrown his leprous tantrum. He simply couldn't believe that Elisha sent a messenger outside to tell him to go dip in the Jordan River seven times. In Naaman's mind, his healing was supposed to be ceremonial, dramatic, and high energy. Yet, Naaman's mind and God's method didn't agree. Therefore, Naaman had a major problem. So what are we to do when God's way of handling our concerns differs from what we think or even ask? First, we must ask ourselves this question: *"Which is more important – how God does it or the mere fact that He does what we need Him to do?"* Look, if you pray for healing, I admit it would be very cool if God performed this miraculous healing that left everyone spellbound. However the key and most important thing is *being healed.* Does it really matter if you have to undergo treatments, endure a little rehab, or take a few pills as long as you're healed? We should celebrate the fact that God IS healing. Our focus should be on the fact that God IS blessing our finances. We should smile about the fact that God IS providing employment. We should be elated that God IS doing great things in our lives. We'll never rid ourselves of the spirit of frustration and anxiety if are always fretting the *process* rather than having faith in God's *promise, power, and providence.* Do you think that Mary and Martha were upset because Jesus called their brother Lazarus from the grave by name instead of going over to the corpse and performing some religious ritual? Absolutely not! I've never read where at the Red Sea Moses told God, *"Ummm, Lord, we need a boat quickly!"* The Bible indicates that Moses wasted no time lifting that rod over the sea. He wasn't concerned with the process. All he sought was God's power and providence. That's how we must be. The seasoned saints often sing a song that says, *"Any way you bless me, Lord, I'll be satisfied."*

    I need to stop here a moment and acknowledge something about what you just finished reading. I realize that when all hell is breaking loose, sometimes it's hard to be positive and keep our focus. That's why it's important that we surround ourselves with people who love us enough to lead us back to the right place—be it physically, spiritually, emotionally, or all three. That's what Naaman's servants did in this text. Look at what they told him. Once again, the Antoyne L. Green version, *"Now look. We have come all the way to Samaria just so you can be healed. What are you upset about, Sir? You were willing to jump through hoops and go through a bunch of changes to be healed! So what's the problem with simply dipping yourself in some water? We don't mean to offend you, but you need to get a grip!"* Likewise, my friend, I don't mean to offend you—but you may need to get a grip! Get a focus! Get over yourself! Swallow your pride! Stop trying to be so deep! Tear up your plan and ask God to show you His! Your blessing, your change, your deliverance, your healing, and all you need is available. In fact, God is ready to do what you need Him to do. In His appointed time, He's going to fulfill every promise He's made to you. However, you've got to be willing to follow His directions. So what if what God says doesn't match your thinking. So what if

God's method and your mind aren't in agreement. We ask God to *show up* and quite honestly, God needs us to *shut up* and *stand up* on our faith in Him! If you can believe a weatherman and his computer as they guess about storms, surely you can believe your God who speaks and storms obey Him.

Yes, I know that it seems like the tenor of my writing just shifted to a strange level of intensity and frankness. It did. We all need people around us that love us enough to tell us like it is—regardless! Too many of us seek those who will *enable* us rather than those who will *empower* us. We must always keep a close check on the company we allow in our intimate space. We all need at least one person who knows how to tell us a few things that we don't want to hear. The people who really want the best for us will tell us that we're wrong. They'll tell us that we're overreacting. They'll tell us we know better. They'll warn us we're messing things up. They'll tell us to be quiet. They'll push us to let some things go. They'll pull us into our neutral corner to cool off rather than push us into the center of the ring to fight it out. Each of us needs someone who can be calm when we're going crazy. We need objective people in our lives that know how to present opposing viewpoints to us that will at least cause us to think some things over. I believe this wholeheartedly: a true friend is willing to momentarily become your enemy if it means doing and saying what's necessary to ensure the very best "you" is on display at all times. This friend would also be brokenhearted if they just sat back and watched you walk, talk, and react your way out of God's blessings. Check your company. It just may be time to downsize your circle.

Eleven: Then...
II Kings 5:14a

"Then went he down..."

Naaman is on the move again. After a temper tantrum and little pouting fit, he's finally headed to the Jordan River. Note that the text says, *"Then went he down..."* The word *"then"* is often overlooked in the passage. However, it's a very important key in understanding Naaman's mentality at the moment. The *"then"* is indicative of a genuine shift in Naaman's mood, emotions, and most of all his thinking. This little word actually helps form the foundation for Naaman's healing.

"Then" indicates that what is being said or done is a result of something that has already been stated or done. So what brought on Naaman's *"then?"* In the last chapter, we discussed how Naaman received wise counsel from his servants. They basically told him to

chill out, grow up, and get to the Jordan. **Then** Naaman went down. The counsel of his servants apparently touched Naaman's heart. As a result, Naaman _received_ the counsel, _recognized_ the error in your thinking and his tantrum, and _responded_ by getting himself together and making his way down to the Jordan River. Naaman had his moment. He unloaded his frustration. **Then,** after being told what was right, he rethought things, refocused, and renewed his resolve to be healed.

Okay, you are hereby given permission to have your moments. Yes, the Pastor is telling you to go ahead scream, kick, holler, huff, puff, stomp, pout, turn red, fold your arms, push your door together with a _little_ extra strength (let's not slam it), cry a little, and play the quiet game with all who are around you. Then when they ask you what's wrong, do what we all do (that would be to lie) and say, *"Nothing!"* It's okay, and even natural, that we have some natural moments when we are hurt, upset, disappointed, and etc. In I Samuel 30, David and his men returned from the battlefield only to find that their city, Ziklag, had been burned and pillaged. Even worse, all of their wives and children were gone. To add insult to injury, all of their possessions had been stolen: the 55" flat screen, PS3 gaming system, the surround sound, iPad, laptop, beds—you name it, it was all gone (okay, I stretched it a bit—but you get the picture). The Word says that David and his 600 men cried until they had no more power to cry. Picture this, warriors who just had the intention of _killing_ were _crying._ It was on only **after** they had their moments that David sought God, got God's approval and directions, and ultimately he and his men went to the Amalekites' camp. There they beat up the enemy all day and all night (boy, that was SOME FIGHT!), and recovered all the Amalekites had stolen from them. However, first David and the boys had to get their emotions out of the way. Know this, we'll never be spiritual, rational, and focused for the task ahead if we're about to explode from emotions. Don't try to be a super saint. Don't try to be ultra-holy. Don't try put on this act like nothing ever affects you. Now, I'm not saying for you to just relegate yourself to being an overly dramatic whiner and worrier. However, I am saying that things happen that get next to us. When these times occur we need to be able to respond in the appropriate way. However, like David and his men, this crying out should have limits. You can't cry and pout forever. *Please* get over some stuff. Eventually you have to release the hurt, refocus, and resolve to recover.

That's exactly what Naaman did. He lost himself. **Then** he came to himself. You remember the prodigal son, don't you? He hit rock bottom. **Then** he came to himself. The prophet Nathan went and told David a story that convicted him of his sins with Bathsheba and against her husband Uriah. **Then** David came to himself. Likewise, things may have gone wrong. **Then** you recognized the wrongs and have a new resolve not to go back down that road again. What you said was rude and inappropriate. Someone you trust called you on it. **Then** you must go and make things right with whomever you offended. You said what you meant and meant what you said. You were sure of what you knew and you stood by it. However, the

Holy Spirit convicted you and let you know that you were so far out in left field with your thinking, words, and actions that you could play for the Atlanta Braves. *Then* you must eat a slice of humble pie, refocus, and move on. You should never allow yourself to be stuck on stupid. Naaman finally remembered that his ultimate goal of being healed from leprosy was still very much a possibility. So he had to move forward. Likewise, we must realize that we haven't touched the tip of the iceberg when it comes to receiving God's promises and realizing our potential in God. There is too much ahead to stay stuck where we are. We should be able to write our <u>*then*</u> testimonies. *Then*...I went ahead and graduated from college. *Then*...I got my finances straight so I'll never fall victim to "get money fast" schemes again. *Then*...I broke off the horrible relationship so that I could finally learn to love myself again. *Then*...I stopped acting like I had no control and finally got focused. *Then*...I stopped listening to all of the negativity and realized that the sky's the limit in what I can do, what I can have, and who can I can be in God. You know, I'm so excited about what God is going to do in my life and your life. I wish I could personally witness all of what God does for you and through you. Hopefully, I will have the privilege of hearing some of your testimonies. In the meantime, just hang in there... ***until THEN.***

Twelve: Persistence during the Process
II Kings 5:14b

"Then went he down, and dipped himself seven times in Jordan, according to the saying of the man of God..."

We can only imagine the range of emotions and thoughts that Naaman had as he was approaching the Jordan River. I'm sure he was probably excited because he believed his bout with leprosy was almost over. Then there could've been a bit of embarrassment because he had leprosy in the first place and because he was about to go and baptize himself in a dirty river in hopes of being healed. To have varying thoughts and emotions while on this faith journey is natural. However, like Naaman, we must rely on our belief and faith in God to keep us pressing forward toward our respective "Jordans." If you haven't grasped anything else in this book, lock in now. I've mentioned earlier that often we forfeit the blessings intended for us because we get impatient and impulsive when <u>God's</u> process challenges <u>our</u> logic, our timing, and our preference as to how things should be done. However, Naaman found out what I hope we'll learn: persistence during God's process pays off.

Can't you just see Naaman finally at the bank of the Jordan River? Take a look through the hidden camera powered by imagination. Observe Naaman as he looks to the left and then to the right. Finally, he begins removing his clothing. First, the big toe dabbles in the water to test the temperature. Then Naaman slides his whole foot into the water. The other foot follows. He proceeds to take a few steps away from the bank of the river—all the while looking around to see if anyone but his servants is watching. He says to himself, *"Well, here it goes."* He pinches his nose, holds his breath, puffs out his cheeks, and *SPLASH!* Naaman dips himself the first time. As soon as he comes up, he looks at his arms, hands, and chest—leprosy is still in full effect. Then he pinches his nose a second time, holds his breath, puffs out his cheeks, and *SPLASH!* After the second dip, Naaman takes another self-exam and finds that his skin is still diseased. He repeats the process a third time, a fourth time, a fifth time, and a sixth time. Still, he was not healed. I just have to believe that though Naaman was certainly acting in faith, he still had some natural thoughts. *"Hmmmm. I'm really looking like a nut doing this over and over again and nothing is happening,"* Naaman may have thought. Or something like this may have crossed his mind, *"I just need to quit doing this, get out of this water, go on back to Syria, and hope things get better."* No doubt the process of deliverance and healing was longer than Naaman would have liked. However, if I could see him now, I'd slap him a big high-five for not giving up and quitting. If he had dipped six times and left the Jordan everything would have been for naught. However, he hung in there and didn't let his emotions and impulses stop him just short of his blessing. Naaman learned that persistence during God's process pays off.

That's the word for you right now. It's possible that you're doing every single thing that you know to do in order to make your situation better. You're following wise counsel. You're following the doctor's orders down to the letter. You've done the project 100% like your boss designed it to be done. You've committed to the changes the marriage counselor suggested. You've embraced a 12-step program AND added three more steps of your own to make sure you're on the right road. Yet, just like Naaman, in the immediate you see absolutely no change. Things still aren't much better. You're still not healed. You've still got the disease. Your boss is still not satisfied. The promotion hasn't come. Your marriage is still on the rocks at best. The steps you've taken to your recovery seem to have taken you in a complete circle and you're right back where you started. So what do you do? Well, the one thing you **_DO NOT_** do is get emotional and then either quit or make impulsive decisions to change the plan set before you. Recently, I was about to launder my dress shirts. Unfortunately, there was an ever-so-slight ring in the collar of my shirt and in the cuffs. In fact, my French Cuffs had transformed into foul cuffs (pray for this preacher)! I decided to pretreat the cuffs with this stuff my wife bought. The instructions said: spray the affected area, rub the chemicals into the stains, and then wash the item of clothing. I did. The stain had lightened; however, it hadn't lifted. So I read the bottle again. The instructions said, *"Heavy stains may require additional treatments. If so, repeat the above instructions."* The Antoyne Green translation: *"If the ring around the collar doesn't come out the first time, then keep treating the stains and washing your shirts until the ring disappears. If you choose not to, just wear a dirty shirt."* Well, I choose not to wear dirty shirts. Therefore, I kept working the <u>process</u> until what I desired, clean shirts, had been delivered. That's what I need to tell you. Keep working the process. Don't give up. Don't give down. Don't give out. Don't give in. You're too close to being debt free. You're too close getting the job. Mr. or Mrs. Right is the way. Your child's acceptance letter into the school or the gifted program will soon be mailed. The sparks are about to be ignited again in your marriage. You're just around the corner from your healing and restoration. PLEASE, my friend, keep working God's process. By the way, the name of the stuff I was treating my shirts with is called *"Totally Awesome!"* This stuff did the trick. Likewise, the one who is going to ensure that our lives are never the same is totally awesome! Trust Him enough to keep plugging way and pressing until "your collar" gets clean.

So what was it that kept Naaman focused. Sure, faith had a lot to do with it. However, it's deeper than that. The text says that Naaman dipped seven times *"according to the saying of the man of God."* Regardless of what Naaman or anyone around him thought or felt, he remained truly obedient to the words of instruction from Elisha. Naaman responded and stayed resilient based on the word released over his life by the prophet. I can imagine Naaman going back and forth within himself out in the Jordan: *"Man, this ain't working. But Elisha said it would. I've dipped six times. That's enough. But Elisha said to dip seven times. Forget it! I'm out of here. But the prophet promised if I do this just like he said I'll be healed. Heck, I'm going to trust Elisha."* Naaman was obedient to the process because he was confident in the promise of healing if he did. We must approach God's instructions in our lives the same way. We must completely sell out to God and trust Him based simply on His Word. In fact, for the believer, at times the Word is all we have to hang our hats on. We can't always depend on others because they have troubles too. We can't depend on our own thinking because there are times trouble in our lives do away with logic. Even when we think clearly, we can't always trust logic because God is not confined to our limited thinking and abilities. We can't depend on our emotions because they tend to run away with us. There are seasons in our lives when all we have to depend on is God's word! In order to live by faith and in the favor of God, we must get comfortable not knowing *how* God's going to work something out. Yet, we trust things *will* work out **because God said so.** You may not be healed yet. Still, trust God's word that He will heal you. You may feel like you're spinning your wheels and nothing is happening. Well, keep spinning. As long as God *promised* to move in your situation, then just buckle up, hunker down, and stay in the *process* until the promise is fulfilled. Remember: we don't walk by understanding or comfort level. We walk by faith.

Thirteen: God Will Do Just What He Says He'll Do
II Kings 5:14

"Then went he down, and dipped himself seven times in Jordan, according to the saying of the man of God: and his flesh came again like unto the flesh of a little child, and he was clean."

It was time for the rubber to meet the road. It was the moment of truth. Naaman dipped the seventh time. Would his skin still be filled with painful, smelly leprous sores or would he be clean? Would Naaman be full of joy or would he be full of anger and frustration? What would the people think? Would they think that he was favored by God or fooled by God? He had done just what he had been instructed to do by the prophet Elisha. God gave Elisha directions and the prophet passed them to Naaman. Naaman did his part. Now would God follow suit? The text gives us the answer very clearly, *"and his flesh came again like unto the flesh of a little child, and he was clean."* God had done just what the prophet Elisha claimed that He would do!

There is no deep, fancy, eloquent, or easier way to say this: our God will do just what He says He'll do. If God says it, it's a done deal! Believe it. Stand on it. Stand by it. Take it the bank. Now, I know that some of us have trust issues. All of us at some point in life have been hurt, let down, misled, deceived, and taken for a ride by some dishonest people. They say one thing and do another. They promise something and never keep the promise. They guarantee something by a certain day and time, only to have others looking like a fool. There's no pretty way to say it: there are some folks out there will lie in a hot minute. They have a lying spirit—it just comes natural to them. Come on, tell the truth and shame the devil (did I really just say that)? We all know some folks that while talking to them on the phone and they're giving all this wonderful information, we're rolling our eyes and shaking our heads. How many times has your mouth said to someone, *"That' is great!*

That's awesome." However, at the same time your heart is saying, *"You really need to quit."* About that time their spirit affects yours and you lie, telling them you have another call coming in, the baby is crying, you're about to leave, and etc. The point is that no man, and I mean *not any* man, should be given our total, complete trust. We're flesh. That means that we're faulty (Romans 3:23). However, the Word says that it's better to trust God than to trust man anyway (Psalm 118:8). God doesn't lie. He's not capable of lying to us (Numbers 23:19). If He says it, He's going to do it! Naaman found that out. Likewise, chances are great that you know this to be true as well. If not, trust me. If God promised it, He'll keep His promise. In His Word, God promised to take care of us. Well, despite what may have happened in your life, you're still here. So He kept His promise. He promised He'll supply our needs. He does it every day. He promised He'll forgive our sins. He does it each time we go to him with a repentant heart and ask Him to. Now, I know that I've just spoken in generalities. However, I've seen specific instances in my life in which God kept His promise to me. I shared with you earlier in this book how our daughter Emani was very sick right after birth. I prayed so hard for her. One night, God awoke me out of my sleep and spoke so softly to me, *"She shall live and not die."* He kept His promise. This little booger is something else! He promised me that my maternal grandmother would live to see at least her 100th birthday. On January 6, 2012, she turned 101 years old. As of the moment I'm writing this chapter of the book (March 20, 2012), she lives with my parents and is still able to get around on her own, with the help of a walker. She's a sharp, spunky lady that loves *"four wangs (her pronunciation of 'wings') and a pie"* from KFC. God kept His promise. The Lord directed me to begin a new ministry back in 2000. On June 4, 2000, the New Life Church began. God promised He would favor the Ministry. He's done just that. Now, many have come. Many have gone. Like any other ministry we've had our share of mountain experiences and only a few valley lows. Still, God kept His promise. Friend, the Bible says that God is not one who shows favorites to people. I'm certainly no more important to God than you are. So if He'll keep His promises to me, He'll certainly keep His promises to you. What does your heart say that God's going to do on your behalf? If He promises healing, get ready to celebrate the healing. If He promises a godly companion, prep yourself to meet him or her. If He promises a better job, get ready for that all important call. If He promises great things in your child's future, get ready to beam like only a proud parent can. If He promises to supply your needs, know that there is no failure in God and you won't go lacking. If God says He's going to restore your mind and spirit, go ahead and serve notice to others not to get used to seeing you the way you are not because a change is coming.

Now, it would be very irresponsible of me to suggest that the promises of God are fulfilled like magic without us having to do anything. I cringe when I see and hear preachers and others pretty much telling people all they have to do is name and claim their blessing. Wrong. I'm here to tell you that you've got to do more than *"reach up and grab"* the blessing. There's more to this walk in God than just speaking a thing into existence. As we've discussed, there is process which leads to God's promises being fulfilled. Naaman had a process to follow to be healed. We also have processes that we must experience in order to ensure God's promise is fulfilled. Naaman experienced God's _supernatural_ power only after Naaman did all he could do and was instructed to do in his _natural_ ability. Okay, let's do it this way. Why would I continue to pray for healing from hypertension if I continue to eat pork chops, bacon, and ribs all the time? Why would I expect God to help me lose weight if I can down a whole pie in 15 minutes? Why do I need God to touch the Human Resources director at any job site so they'll hire me if the truth is I'm as lazy as a fat dog on a porch in the summer heat? Why do I need God to bless me with $1,000.00 dollars and I keep misspending the $100.00 He gives me? You get it. In order for God's power to be seen in our lives, we must want to participate in our own miracles. If Naaman doesn't dip, he doesn't get delivered. So, are you willing to participate in your own miracle? That means, doing everything God directs you to do. It also means exhausting every ounce of your ability in the proper way to effect change in your life. This may mean backing away from the dinner table. It may mean taking your lunch to work instead of eating out all the time in order to save money. It may be time to give the benediction to so-called friends who negatively affect your thinking and decisions. That's when we can expect God to move on our behalf.

Our daughter Jasmynn is quite the basketball player. Yeah, I'm proud to say that she's got game. However, there is so much room for improvement. For the longest, I've stayed on her about getting out and working on her dribble, on her shot, her free throws, and other aspects of the game. Most of the time, I've been met with indifference and a ho-hum attitude. Finally, I left it alone. Well, recently I've noticed she's been outdoors really grinding—working hard for hours. That has prompted me to put on my shoes and go out and help her as much as I can. Because she finally is showing interest in her own development and is willing to participate in her growth, Daddy is excited about helping. In the same manner, when you and I finally strap on our shoes and work hard at the fundamentals of life in Christ, our heavenly Daddy gets excited. That's when He does all that is necessary to bless us, change us, deliver us, and make our lives so much better. It's not on God. It's all on us.

Fourteen: Go Back to God
II Kings 5:15a

"And he returned to the man of God, he and all his company, and came, and stood before him…"

Naaman looks at his skin. It's clean and soft. God has healed him. Man, what a relief it must have been to simply be Naaman again and not Naaman the leper. Again, through the eyes of imagination, let's picture Naaman. Can't you see him walking out of the water, drying off, and then picking up the Vaseline Intensive Care so he can take care of his "new skin?" Then he puts on his clothes, grabs his belongings, and then starts walking—almost jogging in a hurried pace. No doubt his servants are screaming, *"Sir, where are you going?"* Naaman never slows down, but hollers over his shoulder, *"I've got to get to Elisha. I need to see the man of God."* Naaman is intent on going back to the one who, through God's directions, got him out of a bad situation. That's a word for anybody who has ever seen

However God Chooses

God do great and impossible things in his or her life. When God gets you out, go back to Him. When God makes a way for you, you make your way back to Him. Here's what I mean. Note the text says that Naaman *"returned to the man of God...and came and stood before him."* The first time Naaman approached Elisha's door, he was *postured to plead* because he had a major problem. This time he returns to the prophet's door in a *posture of praise*. Naaman teaches us that if you can go to God (or anyone else, for that matter) to beg, then once He shows Himself mighty and strong in your situation, the least you can do is go back to bless Him. I'll never forget once I was traveling quite a bit and my lawn was grossly neglected. I mean that it looked so bad that it could've been mistaken for the wilderness. Heck, I was expecting the children of Israel to come marching from my yard to the back porch at any moment. Yet, I simply didn't have the time to mow the lawn. So I called my dad and asked him to come over and mow it for me. The next day I came home and noticed that my yard looked great. Then I got busy and focused on other things. Finally a day or two passed and my dad called me and said, *"Seems to me if you could call me and ask me to do something for you, common decency says you'll call me back and acknowledge I did it."* That's the word to you from our Heavenly Father.

It's all about telling our Heavenly Father *"thank you."* If you prayed to Him to deal with the mess you were in, then go back and praise Him after He brings you out of the mess. If you called His name in sincere prayer when you didn't know how you were going to make it, then call His name again and say, *"Thank you"* when you know that God kept you, provided for you, and strengthened you in some of the toughest days of your life. After the successful surgery, shout! After closing the important business deal, clap your hands and celebrate. When the jury decides in your favor, find a quiet moment to tell *THE Judge*, "Thank you." I remember a gospel song from a few years back that keeps me in a mode of thanksgiving. Its lyrics say, *"As good as God has been to me, I can't afford not to praise His name. As good as God has been to me, I'm going to give Him the highest praise."* David says in Psalm 34:1, *"I will bless the Lord at all times: his praise shall continually be in my mouth."* Wow! I've messed around and gotten excited at this keyboard! David penned these words right after he was delivered from hand of Abimelech. Do you know what he really was saying in this text? Let me translate for you, *"There ain't no time that God won't know how much I thank Him!"* Likewise, the moment God does something for you—great or small—be intentional on going back to Him. That is, seek a time of intimate fellowship with Him—just to tell Him, "Thanks." However, I must warn you of something. Your private praise moment may stay in your spirit and subsequently could erupt into a public display at any time. You may be at Wal-Mart and throw up your hand in praise. You may be at a restaurant and feel the need to bow your head and shed a tear. You may be in a gathering and just smile or laugh for no apparent reason. Then possibly a simple conversation with someone may turn into a testimony period and praise break. When people ask you what's wrong, just tell them *"Nothing! There just ain't no time that God won't know how much I thank Him."*

Fifteen: So They Will Know
II Kings 5:15a

"And he returned to the man of God, he and all his company, and came, and stood before him…"

Naaman didn't return to Elisha's home alone. The text indicates that *"he and his company"* made the trek. You've got to give credit to Naaman's servants and other traveling companions for standing by him. From the moment they left Syria until reaching Elisha's home the second time, these folks never left his side. I know what you may be thinking. Servants didn't have much of a choice but to be there. I got that. However, I believe they truly cared for Naaman. They could've been servants without offering him wise counsel when he was about to lose his mind the first time at Elisha's house. While Naaman was playing *"This Is the Way I Dip Myself,"* the servants could've left him. What we see here epitomizes what it means to have faithful friends. It's safe to say they were with

Naaman in Syria before he got sick. They never left his side after he became a leper. They traveled with him to Samaria. They talked some sense into him when needed. They apparently were around when he was in the Jordan. They witnessed his healing. Then they traveled with him back to the Prophet Elisha's home. If that's not faithfulness and loyalty, I don't know what is. It is sad to say, but most of us have many acquaintances, but few true friends. A true friend will be there with you and for you regardless of what life throws at you and where life takes you. They'll love you when all is well and when all is wrong. They'll be there for you when it appears everyone is for you and when it feels like everyone has turned on you. True friends will celebrate with you and also pull out a Kleenex and cry with you. They'll stand at the marriage altar with you and in divorce court as well. They'll be in the doctor's office for the diagnosis, in the hospital for the surgery, in the pharmacy getting your medicines after the surgery, and in your home doing whatever is needed while you recoup. If you have people in

Antoyne L. Green

your corner that, good or bad, high or low, big bank account or broke, healthy or sickly, right or wrong they're always there—then you have something to praise God for. Like these people in Naaman's circle, true friends don't always agree with you. They also refuse to enable you when you're functioning below what's logical, rational, and practical. However, they love you enough to talk to you and pray for you. Then they'll be there when you need them the most. So, are most of the people around you *friends or acquaintances?*

I don't believe that Naaman was the only one who benefitted from loyal people around him. His servants and friends also benefitted by seeing firsthand what God could do. They knew leprosy had wreaked havoc on Naaman. They knew his pain. They knew the horrible condition of his skin. No doubt after convincing Naaman to go on and dip in the Jordan River, they stood on the riverbank and watched him as he baptized himself. After the seventh dip, I'm sure they were probably amazed that Naaman's leprous skin was as good as new. The servants, friends, and others loyal to Naaman witnessed with their own eyes how obedience to God and faith in God pays off. They saw how the power of God can change the most impossible and improbable situation. In other words, Naaman's difficulties served as a billboard for God's power to deliver. His tragedy was an advertisement for how God's power can turn things around for our good.

On April 27, 2011, the Southeast was ravaged by killer tornados. Several twisters struck here in North Alabama. It was a daylong event that, when it was finally over, destruction was everywhere. About a mile from my home, complete neighborhoods were destroyed. Also destroyed was the Bethel Church of Christ. This modest-sized church has been in Athens-Limestone County for decades. However, it was reduced to mere rubble that day. Recently, I was traveling down one of the local streets and passed by this monstrous, elaborate, and almost breathtaking building that's under construction. It looked like a church, but I wasn't sure. I stopped just to look around and discovered that this was Bethel's new building. My God! It just reaffirmed to me just how God can take the most tragic scenarios and turn them in God-success stories. He took broken pieces and turned them into a better Bethel. Now, I don't know one single person that goes to that Church. However, being a pastor myself, their situation continues to minister to me right now. Bethel "advertises" for God in this sense: God specializes in restoration. That's true in buildings, lives, finances, emotions—you name it. The seasoned saints used to say, *"If I was never sick, I'd never know that God can heal."*

Speaking of healing, I have to tell you about one miraculous story. There is a deacon in my church named Hillard Smith. He and his wife, Dora, travel about 45 miles one way each Sunday to attend worship at New Life. You'll never meet more faithful and loyal people as these two wonderful people. Deacon Smith had worked a couple of decades for the State Highway Department. One day he was at work driving down a major state highway. It was raining hard when somehow he lost control of

However God Chooses

his vehicle. Hillard spun off of the road and down an embankment. He was thrown from the truck and landed in a wet ravine. I'll never forget receiving the call telling me about the accident and that my good deacon was being airlifted to a local trauma unit. I picked up Elder Causten Meaux (another very loyal member) and we rushed to the hospital. We got to the emergency room and identified ourselves. Immediately the nurses took us back to his trauma bay. Nothing, and I mean nothing, could prepare us for what we were about to see. Deacon Smith was swollen, battered, bruised, and cut on just about every part of his body. His face looked as if he were wearing a Spiderman mask. There were just that many cuts, scrapes, and scratches on his face. He was bleeding everywhere. Dora was standing there, trying to keep her husband calm. All the while she was trying to stay calm herself. In all my years of being a pastor, I had never experienced anything like this. I thought, *"My deacon is about to die in front of my eyes."* I said the right things. I remained calm. However, I was heartbroken and scared to death. The only thing I knew to do was pray. I grabbed Hillard's bloody hand and just began to pray. As I called the name of Jesus, the good deacon began to utter, through a mouth that continually filled with blood, *"Yes, Jesus! Yes, Jesus!"* Dora cried, *"Please, Jesus. Have mercy, Master."* After finishing the prayer, Elder Meaux and I went to the waiting room and sat quietly. I knew just any moment the doctor would come with the news I both dreaded and expected, *"I'm sorry. We lost him."* Finally, after a couple of hours we left. Still, I expected the horrible midnight phone call. It never happened that night, or the next night, or the next night, or the next night.

Somehow Deacon Smith survived. He spent weeks in Intensive Care on a ventilator. He couldn't eat. He couldn't drink anything for real. I remember visiting him and watching Dora swab his mouth with a lemon flavored sponge just to alleviate the intense dry mouth Hillard had. Time went on and eventually the ventilator was removed. However, my deacon couldn't walk. He couldn't move his arms. Nothing.

Eventually Deacon Smith was transferred to rehab in Atlanta. At first, things didn't go so well. I dreaded visiting him and actually put it off for a while. Finally, several members of the Church loaded a van and went to Atlanta to see our friend. When we walked in, I was shocked in a very good way. Deacon was talking, driving his hotrod wheelchair, and giving orders to the nurses and staff. The Lord had literally brought this man from the brink of death. Now, he was still very weak and had a long, intense road to go. However, it was a miracle just to see him. Months and months passed. Then one Sunday, the back doors of our sanctuary opened. Here comes Deacon Smith rolling into the Church. Needless to say, the Church came unglued with intense and radical praise and worship. Today, Smith is walking, has increased movement of his arms, talks like a champ, eats like a champ, and is active in the ministry. He and Dora are a blessing to all of us who know this story. They are God's poster kids for *"Miracles by the Master."* The New Life FAMILY and I are just blessed to be a part of their company. We witnessed the devastation. However, we were blessed to also see Deacon Smith's deliverance. We saw firsthand the pain. Now, the Smiths are living testimonies of how God's power is seen in our pain and how He can fix what's broken. This incident that Hillard and Dora Smith endured was not only for their spiritual growth, but also so all of us who love them would know that God is able to do ANYTHING and EVERYTHING we need Him to do.

So the next time you deal with your trial and test, keep one thing in mind. You're going to grow and learn from it. However, when others see how God moves in your life—how He heals, how He brings peace in the midst of storms, how He provides, and how He turns midnights into miracles—they'll know that the God you serve is great, powerful, and mighty.

Sixteen: So YOU Will Know
II Kings 5:15b

"And he returned to the man of God, he and all his company, and came, and stood before him: and he said, Behold, now I know that there is no God in all the earth, but in Israel…"

It is one thing for others to testify about what God has done for you. It's another thing for you to be a living testimony of just how good God has been. No one can tell your story like you can. While others may have witnessed what happened in your life from the outside, only you know the depth and the power it really took to pull you through some of life's most daunting and difficult times. In the case of Naaman, we've just discussed how his servants and traveling companions were eyewitnesses to how God healed the leper. To a degree they knew Naaman's state of mind after having ministered to him just to convince him to go dip in the Jordan River as instructed. However, nobody knew all that went through this man's mind. No one had a frustration meter attached to him to know just how close he was to really blowing his top. Nobody had the intimate insight to know how close Naaman was to his breaking point. Who could tell what Naaman was really thinking while dipping in Jordan? Naaman was surrounded by people; yet he was still very much isolated in many regards. That's why after being delivered from leprosy, only Naaman could truly testify about what God had done for him. In the same light, only you <u>really</u> know the extremes of your story. That's why only you can truly give God the glory He deserves after He shows Himself strongly on your behalf.

Naaman gets to Elisha's home, knocks on the door, stands before the prophet and then excitedly says, *"Behold, now I know that there is no God in all the earth, but in Israel."* This kind of struck me at first because way back in verse one when we were introduced to Naaman, it says *"but by [Naaman] the Lord had given deliverance unto Syria."* At least on the surface, it appeared that Naaman had some sort of relationship with

God because the Lord had been on his side while leading the Syrian army in battle. So why, after the bout with leprosy, is Naaman saying *"…now I know that there is no God in all the earth, but in Israel?"* There are three key words here: *NOW I KNOW*. You see—there is a difference in knowing *of* someone and *actually* knowing them personally. There is a difference in encountering someone and actually engaging that person. When I was a television reporter in Birmingham, I covered the story when President Bill Clinton came to town. I encountered him. I even shook his hand. However, I have never engaged him personally on a deeper level. In the same manner, we can be around the Church, even read and believe some Scriptures, and know all the religious jargon there is without having a real, meaningful relationship with God. It's possible to hear what God can and will do without knowing Him for yourself. Naaman had been told he'd be healed if got to the prophet in Samaria. The slave girl first stated this. Then Elisha said it as well. However, it was only after dipping seven times and coming up healed of leprosy could Naaman finally say, *"Now I KNOW"* this God is real. It took the problem, the process, and the providence of God before Naaman could testify about God from a personal experience.

I believe that some seasons of struggle are divinely orchestrated to deliver us from bootlegged testimonies. It's so easy to shout about God being a healer if you've never been sick. It's easy to proclaim Him as a provider when you've never lacked for anything. It is good religious speak to say our Lord is a great friend when you're consistently surrounded by those who seem to love you so much. When all is working well, it doesn't take much for us to tell everybody how good God is. While one may truly believe these statements, his testimony is superficial, at best, if he has never truly experienced God in these capacities. However, if you're a cancer survivor, survived the strokes, made it through the risky surgery, and have made some remarkable recovery from illness—be it physical, mental, or emotional—you can say *NOW I KNOW* that God is a healer. If you've had more _due_ bills than dollar bills, yet someway and somehow your bills got paid, you can say *NOW I KNOW* that God is Jehovah-Jireh, my Provider. It's only after people turn on you, betray you, or walk off and leave you that you can truly say *NOW I KNOW* that Jesus is a real friend that will stick and stay regardless of the situation. Your testimony only becomes truly valid after you've endured some tests in which only God brought you through.

Notice the last part of Naaman's statement. He basically told Elisha, *"I've found out there this no God like the God of Israel. He's the real deal."* The seasoned saints used to sing these lyrics, *"There are some things I may not know. There are some places that I may not go. But there is one thing I am sure of. My God is REAL, for I can feel Him deep in my soul."* Friend, it has taken me a couple of weeks of writing, sixteen chapters, and a little more than 100 pages to finally get to the four words this book is really all about: **OUR GOD IS REAL!** Bless His Holy name! Gospel songwriter and singer Vashawn Mitchell has a popular song out right now that says, *"I searched* *all over – couldn't find nobody. I searched high and low – still couldn't find nobody. Nobody's greater. Nobody's greater. Nobody's greater than you."* This is really a love song to a REAL God. Do you agree with Vashawn Mitchell? After our God kept you from losing your mind in the middle of some stormy seasons, were you convinced nobody's greater than our God? After our God put your life back on track after a hurtful divorce – or kept your marriage from divorce – you know that nobody's greater than our God. After the Lord has extended so much grace and mercy to us when He could've (and probably should've) lowered the boom on us, we all should testify that nobody's greater than our God. When we consider all the wrongs and bad decisions we've made in our lives, yet God forgave us, *"Nobody's Greater"* should be our anthem. When you had little or no help raising your precious babies, yet they are strong, healthy, and on their way to bright futures – you should holler NOBODY'S GREATER than my God. Okay, none of those examples worked for you. Well if this one doesn't, I think we have a problem: when you think of how God sent His Son Jesus Christ to die for us so Hell would not be our eternal home, how Jesus was buried in a borrowed tomb, but right early (uh oh, the Baptist preacher is starting to leak… smile) on the third appointed morning Jesus arose from the dead—somebody, anybody, everybody who is saved should have a "NOBODY'S GREATER" testimony. There's a chant we often say that's very appropriate right now, *"When I think of the goodness of Jesus and all He's done for me, my soul cries out Hallelujah. I thank God for saving me."* Is that your testimony?

Whew! Let me stop for minute. See ya in Chapter 17…

Antoyne L. Green

Seventeen: Release after You Receive
II Kings 5:15c

*"...now therefore I pray thee,
take a blessing of thy servant."*

Back in 2001, my wife and I went on a cruise with my sister and brother-in-law. We were on a huge, beautiful boat with just about every amenity imaginable—even a brand spanking new casino. Well, let me go ahead and set the record straight: no, the Preacher Man is not a gambler. I value my money way too much to risk it wastefully. Nine times out of ten, the risks of gambling far outweigh its rewards. HOWEVER, I was intrigued to go to the casino and go a few rounds with Lady Luck. So I set a maximum amount that I would gamble. I made up my mind that win, lose, or draw when I exhausted that dollar amount I would quit. So, I got my ten dollars in quarters (mmmm hmmm, you just knew I was talking big money) and headed to the casino. All I wanted to do was play the slots, the one-armed bandits. I quickly put quarter after quarter into the machine. I won nothing. I had spent about eight of my ten dollars when I pulled the arm again. Bells went off. Sirens blared. Then suddenly a flood of quarters poured from the machine. I had won $50.00. Quit? Heck no! Yep, it was time to double and maybe even triple my money. I started dumping quarters in the slot like a madman. After losing about fifteen bucks, it hit me. Though I had lucked up and won a few minutes ago, chances were great that in just a few minutes I'd be upset because I'd end up giving the machine far more than it would ever give me. That wasn't fair. That wasn't cool. So I stopped giving it my quarters and left. Let me ask you something. What if God felt the same way about us? What if He felt that He gives far more than we ever even attempt to give Him? What if He decided that He'd done enough? So in turn, He'd leave us alone? Oh, how horrible that would be. I know, somebody is reading this and saying, *"Antoyne, what could I possibly give to*

God? He made everything. Everything is His." You're right. However, there is something that you can give to God that is so valuable to Him. He wants YOU. You and I, and every human being, are far more precious to God than every other creation He's made. God has an Uncle Sam mentality. He says, *"I just want YOU!"*

Naaman shows us what it means to celebrate the blessing of God by being selfless and considerate of the one who blessed him. After giving his testimony about how awesome God was, Naaman says to Elisha (Antoyne Version), *"Sir, you've been so good to me! Now, please allow me to bless you in return."* Remember, Naaman had in his possession a boatload of silver, gold, and ten different sets of clothing. He wanted Elisha to have the majority of these things because he, the prophet, was used of God to heal him. Naaman refused to receive the blessing of healing and not release a blessing back to the one who made the difference in his life. We must have the same attitude. Whenever anyone blesses us—whether it is a friend, our parents, our pastor, our Church FAMILY, our co-workers, or whomever—we should be selfless enough to WANT to bless them in a special way. Sow a financial seed. Take someone to lunch. Offer to do something special for them. In the very least, give them a big hug and express just how much you appreciate them. You'd be surprised that many people are blessed more by true, sincere, and loving words than anything else. When you receive a blessing, release a blessing.

That's certainly the case when it comes to God. As God releases things to our lives, we should release our lives back to God. That's what really blesses our Lord. You can't pay God for what He does. There is not one thing we can give God physically that He doesn't already have. However, the one thing we can do that will move the heart of God and make our Father smile is to worship Him. Earlier, we talked about how praising God is necessary, and certainly in order. Our praise is the acknowledgment of what God has done for us—the new car, the healing, the scholarship, the new home, waking us up. We praise God for anything and everything God does in our lives. However, worship is different because it acknowledges the _person_ of God. Worship says to our Father, *"This is who you are to me."* You may be saying, *"Okay, I understand worship, but how does that equate to giving God something? How do I give myself to God in worship?"* You see, true worship can't happen until there is a complete, purposeful focus on God. True worship comes from a clear mind and a pure heart. True worship is intentional because phones will be turned off, televisions will be black, iPods and iPads aren't being manipulated, and no one else is given attention. Worship seeks the heart of God and says, *"Lord, here I am. I want to experience your presence. I give you my heart, my mind, my spirit, and every bit of my existence. Nothing else matters but you. No one else matters but you. This moment is given to no one else but you."* So we must _seek_ God in our worship.

Then we must _salute_ God in our worship. Who doesn't like to hear others speak highly of them? Who doesn't like to be reaffirmed by those who love them? God is no different in this regard. He loves it when His people give themselves to Him in worship and the give Him glory and honor by acknowledging who He is to them. Now, while worship and praise are different, they are related. Often our worship is born out of our praise. You see, whatever God does for you will become the foundation for who He is to you. If He has provided for you in any way, you praise Him for the provisions. However, when you think about how He provided for you financially, gave you a job, and opened doors you worship God as Jehovah-Jireh—which means, "my Provider." When He's healed you, in worship you thank Him for being Jehovah-Raphe, your Healer. When He kept you from breaking into pieces during some rough times and gave you His peace, you can passionately thank Him for being Jehovah-Shalom, which means "our peace." You get it. Worship is all about being intimate with God to the point that all you do is state to Him—with a heart of love and thanksgiving—all He's been and all He is to you. If He's been your friend, tell Him so. If He's been your confidant, let Him know it. If He's been your company keeper, acknowledge it. If He's been your protector and shield, don't hesitate to whisper that acknowledgment to Him in worship. While Naaman offered Elisha physical goods, He could have easily worshiped God as his guide, his encourager, his peace, and his healer. Yes, the maid told Naaman's wife about Elisha. Yes, Syria's king sent him to Samaria. Yes, Elisha told him to dip seven times. Yes, Naaman's servants convinced him to do it. Yes, he dipped in the Jordan. However, God orchestrated every step of this journey. Furthermore, the healing came from God. No one or nothing else healed Naaman. Never mistake this, anything good that happens to you is the result of divine providence. The banker that said "yes," when he really shouldn't have, was a result of God touching hearts. The boss hiring you when others were more qualified was a result of God touching minds. The unexpected check or financial blessing was the result of God doing great things. The forgiveness you received from someone dear to you was the result of God softening hearts with His mercy. There is not one thing that happens to us positively that is not from God. Therefore, we never should run out of passion and reasons to worship God.

Finally, releasing yourself to God is all about surrendering totally and completely to His will. Friend, I have no clue what all God has in store for you. Yet, I'm confident that your best days are ahead. However, I can assure you that you'll never receive the very best God has to offer if you're not willing to release all of your being to Him. This means your time, your talent, your treasure, your talk, your thinking, your body—your EVERYTHING for His service. In the Model Prayer, we pray *"Thy will be done."* Well, God's will can't be done until our wills are diminished. No, God's will is not always comfortable. The Master's will is not without some painful moments. Our Father's will sometimes doesn't make a lick of sense to us. However, must pray for the spirit of surrender in all things. We must basically pray the lyrics of a song we used to sing a long time ago, *"I'm yours, Lord. Everything I am. Everything I'm not. Everything I've got. I'm yours, Lord. Try me and see.*

See if I won't be completely yours." Then another song touches my heart, *"Yes, Lord. Yes, Lord. From the bottom of my heart, to the depths of my soul, yes Lord. Completely yes — my soul says yes!"* If you can honestly and truly say and pray these words to our God—then you have a spirit of surrender. However, it's more than that. Daily we must ask God to keep our minds on Him. We must ask Him not to allow us to follow our flesh and be driven by our emotions. We must be insistent on not allowing our company to corrupt our focus. Instead, daily we must continue to say, *"I'm yours Lord."* Even when it gets hard and we don't understand what's going on or what's going to happen, we still must whisper to God, *"Yes, Lord."* I promise you that once we get to this point in our lives, we'll live in the full confidence of knowing that God will always be there for us. Our hearts will always be content in knowing that every situation will work out for our good. We just have to allow God to be the Sovereign God that He is in our lives. When we do, we'll simply say, *"Lord, I don't understand everything. In fact, at times, I personally wish things would work out differently. Yet, I surrender to your will and way. Therefore, God bless me however You choose."*

www.ingramcontent.com/pod-product-compliance
Lightning Source LLC
Chambersburg PA
CBHW061440040426
42450CB00007B/1141